FATHERCARE

BOOKS BY CHARLES PAUL CONN

Biography:
The New Johnny Cash
No Easy Game (with Terry Bradshaw)
Kathy (with Barbara Miller)
Julian Carroll of Kentucky
Hooked on a Good Thing (with Sammy Hall)
Just off Chicken Street (with Floyd McClung)
Battle for Africa (with Brother Andrew)

Inspirational:
Making It Happen
Believe! (with Richard M. DeVos)
The Magnificent Three (with Nicky Cruz)
FatherCare

Business:
The Possible Dream
The Winner's Circle
An Uncommon Freedom

FATHERCARE

WHAT IT MEANS
TO BE GOD'S CHILD

CHARLES PAUL CONN

WORD BOOKS
PUBLISHER
WACO, TEXAS

A DIVISION OF
WORD, INCORPORATED

FATHERCARE: WHAT IT MEANS TO BE GOD'S CHILD

Scripture quotations used in this book are from the following sources:
The New Testament in Modern English (Phillips), translated by J. B. Phillips. © J. B. Phillips, 1958, 1960, 1972.
The Revised Standard Version of the Bible (RSV), copyrighted 1946, 1952, © 1971 and 1973 by the Division of Christian Education of the National Council of the Churches of Christ in the U.S.A.
The King James Version of the Bible (KJV).
Today's English Version of the Bible (TEV) © American Bible Society 1966, 1971, 1976.
The New English Bible (NEB), © The Delegates of the Oxford University Press and The Syndics of the Cambridge University Press, 1961, 1970.
The New International Version of the Bible (NIV), copyrighted © 1973 the New York Bible Society International.
The New American Standard Bible (NAS) © The Lockman Foundation 1960, 1962, 1968, 1971.
The Holy Bible: An American Translation (Beck), translated by William F. Beck (New Haven, MO: Leader Publishing Co., 1976).

ISBN 0-8499-0339-4

Printed in the United States of America

To
RAYMOND CONN,
my brother,
with whom I enjoy
not only the bond of our shared family,
but also that of a kindred spirit.

Contents

Preface

This is a simple book about a simple idea.

The most important ideas, especially those having to do with God, are often the simplest ones. J. B. Phillips, the great scholar and Bible translator, once warned, "Let us be on our guard against that common human tendency to elaborate a simple issue. We should be continually vigilant against complicating the simplicity of our faith, or before long the simple walk with God becomes such a complicated spiritual exercise that the Good News ceases to be good. I do not claim that Christianity is easy; I do claim that it is not complicated."

Our attempts to explain God often obscure more than they illuminate. It is possible, in our search for more novel insights into God's nature, to ignore His simplest and most basic quality—His willingness to care for us as His little children. This book points us back toward that view of God.

In my own search for an honest sense of intimacy with God, this old-fashioned idea of Him as a loving parent has been of enormous value. Particularly as I am becoming a more experienced parent myself, I am learning firsthand something of what FatherCare involves, and in the process am

Preface

finding my heavenly Father more understandable. My hope is that these reflections on what it means to be God's child will be helpful to you also.

In even a small volume such as this one, there are those who must be thanked. My appreciation goes to Floyd Thatcher and Ernie Owen, my editors at Word Books, who encouraged me to put these thoughts on paper, and to Anne Christian Buchanan for her excellent editorial assistance. Also to my fellow worshipers at the Westmore Church of God, with whom I have shared them in a different form. My thanks to Don Bowdle for his help with the Greek.

The illustrations used here are drawn from my own family life, and that necessarily involves a certain intrusion into the privacy of my parents, my brothers and sisters, and my children. I am deeply grateful to them all for the richness of our family life together, and I appreciate their allowing this use of our shared memories.

In more than the ordinary sense, my wife, Darlia, has been a part of this book. We have often discussed these ideas, and have tried together to put them into practice. I must thank her for the joy I have in being her partner, as together we seek to be better parents of our three children, and to be better children, ourselves, in the family of God.

CHARLES PAUL CONN

1

God Draws Us a Picture

"Our Father which art in heaven . . ."
Matthew 6:9, KJV

God wants us to understand Him—so much that He drew us a picture.

He has drawn us several pictures, in fact, in an effort to show us how He feels about us, and how we should feel about Him. They are word pictures, and they are contained in the Bible. Perhaps more effectively than any other part of that extraordinary Holy Book, these word pictures help us to know what God is like and how we can relate to Him.

Jesus Christ understood how difficult it can be for a finite human being to understand an infinite God. When He spoke of the ways of God, He spoke in simple terms, in stories and illustrations which came from the everyday lives of the people who listened to Him. His purpose was not to establish a formal and complex theology, but to clearly communicate a simple message. He realized that every person in every age looks for the answers to the same set of questions: What is God like? What do I mean to Him? What does God see when He looks at me? What does He expect of me, and what can I expect of Him?

Jesus answered those questions by drawing pictures—familiar word pictures which everyone understood.

"You are like a light on a lampstand," He said.

"Look at the birds in the sky," He said. "They never sow nor reap nor store away in barns, and yet they are fed."

"Don't look at the speck of sawdust in your brother's eye and ignore the plank in your own," He said.

"Everyone who hears these words and practices them is like a sensible man who builds his house on the rock," He said.

His preaching was never intended to dazzle or impress, but always to communicate. No doubt His approach would be dismissed by many modern theologians and church leaders as shallow and superficial, because He relied so heavily upon such simple anecdotes. Even in His day, He was underestimated by the scholarly and analytical churchmen of that time. Some considered His style too popular and simplistic to be regarded as a serious and substantive message.

But the ordinary people who heard Jesus realized that for the first time they were beginning to understand God. "When Jesus had finished these words," Matthew reported, "the crowd were astonished at the power behind His teaching. For His words had the ring of authority . . ." (Matt. 7:28, Phillips).

Of the many word pictures which Christ drew to explain God, there are two which appear frequently. Both occur not only in the teachings of Jesus, but throughout the Old and New Testaments. One of these is the metaphor of God as a Shepherd and us as His sheep. The other is that of God as a Parent and us as His children.

Both these illustrations are used in Scripture to describe the relationship between God and man. Both convey a message about that unique interaction which would be difficult to communicate in the more formal vocabulary of a doctrinal statement. They are richly textured metaphors that evoke from us not only an intellectual, but also an emotional, response as we understand God through them.

Of the two, however, the shepherd-and-sheep analogy is considerably more culture-bound. It obviously lies closer to the experience of the typical person in the first-century Jewish culture than to that of a twentieth-century American. Most contemporary Christians, in fact, rarely have seen a flock of grazing sheep, much less shepherds tending them. Very few of us have ever actually *been* a shepherd, and none of us will ever be a sheep!

The parent-and-child analogy, on the other hand, is as fresh in one century as in another, no matter how the times and culture change. Parents and children are forever; the dynamics of their relationship are timeless. Whatever else may change, the emotion a mother has when she looks

into her baby's face, the feeling of a father for his
growing son—those things never change. And
further, all of us have first-hand experience of at
least part of that parent-child relationship. Many of
us have been parents, and all of us have been
children!

Perhaps that is why God uses this universally
understood relationship as His most powerful device
to tell us about Himself.

Consider another important difference between
the shepherd-and-sheep model and the parent-and-
child one. The view of God as Parent and us as His
sons and daughters is more than just a descriptive
device. It is not merely an illustration; it is a literal
and real relationship. We understand, as we read
Psalm 23, that we are not *literally* sheep, nor God a
Shepherd. But the view of God as a Father is not
only a beautifully poetic way of looking at Him; it is
truly and literally what He is! We are not actually
salt, lights on a hill, sheep, nor grass in the field,
though Jesus compares us to them to help us
understand the Kingdom. But we are indeed His
children, in reality as well as in metaphor.

Perhaps it is the very familiarity of the parent-
child relationship which keeps us from taking it
more seriously as a model by which to know better
how to relate to God. Sometimes in looking for the
mysteries of God we overlook the obvious lessons
which lie closest to our own everyday experience.

It is possible to make that mistake with this
simple way of coming into a more intimate
relationship with God. We should not assume it is
such a familiar word picture that it has no more to
teach us. It is tempting to charge straight past the

valuable lessons of this biblical model as we search for more exotic sources of inspiration. But the fact that God leaned so heavily on the parent-child example in the Old and New Testaments indicates it must undoubtedly contain a rich lode of insight, and it is unlikely we have uncovered all that is there. So let's take a new look at the old message that God is a Parent and we are His sons and daughters.

2

Twice His Children

"But to all who received him . . . he gave
power to become children of God."
John 1:12, RSV

When I was a child, a favorite Sunday school
story was a simple parable called "Little Boat Twice
Owned." In the story, a young boy was given a toy
which he particularly enjoyed, a small wooden boat
which he sailed at the end of a string in the ponds
and streams where he played. One day the string
broke, and the boat floated away and was lost.

Several days later, as the story goes, the child
spotted his boat in the display window of a used-toy
store. It was unmistakably his own—same colors,
same scars in the wooden finish. Without doubt it
was the very boat he had lost. The youngster dashed
into the shop to inquire about it. The boat had been
found several miles away, he was told, and the
storeowner had bought it from the man who

retrieved it. It was to be resold for a modest price. The boy was delighted at the unexpected chance to regain possession of this favorite of all his toys. Asking the shopkeeper to put the battered little boat aside for him, he hurried home, emptied his piggy bank, and returned with a fistful of coins with which to buy it.

The little boy afterward loved the toy more than ever because it was *twice* his—originally as a gift, and a second time chosen and purchased by himself.

Becoming a child of God is a similar two-step process. In a sense we are all God's children. Men and women everywhere—of whatever religion or none at all—are God's children in the most basic sense. Remember the chorus the preschoolers sing?

Jesus loves the little children,
All the children of the world;
Red and yellow, black and white;
They are precious in His sight.
Jesus loves the little children of the world.

As individual creatures of God, made in His image, we are all children of God, whether we know Him in a personal way or not. We are His children in something like a "genetic" sense, in the sense that He is our Source. Every person who has ever lived issues from God. We are His creative offspring, and He is therefore our Father from the moment we are born. One need not be a believing Christian, nor acknowledge God in any way at all, to be God's child in that sense.

But the Bible clearly shows that it is possible to be God's child in an entirely different way, a deeper and more personal way. There is a second sense in which He is a Father to us, and this experience of being God's child is richer than merely having been created by Him. This second level is one in which we interact with God as child to Father and He relates to us in the warmly personal role of a loving Parent. It is an intimate relationship based on the familiar *functions* and roles of parent and child. In this sense, we have a Father whom we know, and whose personal love and support we experience on a daily basis. We are His children not merely in the broad and cosmic sense that He created us, but in a constant interchange in which He does for us the things natural fathers do for children they love.

It is this richer level of childhood toward which Scripture points us. It is one thing to realize logically that, having been born, I must therefore have somewhere a father who, in a fashion, produced me. It is quite another thing to know my father personally, closely—to live in his house, eat at his table, and feel his arm around my shoulders on a day-to-day basis.

Being a child of God in such a way is possible, but it does not occur automatically. It is not part of the universal condition. It must be chosen by each individual—specifically and decisively chosen. One *becomes* God's child—not just His creature, but His child—and in that moment begins to experience the parenthood of God in a new dimension. John describes it this way: "But to all who received him, who believed in his name, he gave power to *become* children of God" (John 1:12, RSV, emphasis mine).

FatterCare

The opportunity to become God's child is a gift which the sacrifice of Jesus Christ made possible. It is the result of God's love for us, and of His determination to redeem us from sin by making us His own personal sons and daughters. He does this by literally adopting us, just as if we were lonely orphans with no one else to care for us. The apostle Paul explained it to the Galatians: "But when the time had fully come, God sent forth his Son . . . so that we might receive adoption as sons. And because you are sons, God has sent the Spirit of his Son into our hearts, crying, 'Abba! Father!' So through God you are no longer a slave but a son, and if a son then an heir" (Gal. 4:4–7, RSV).

In another passage, Paul reminds us that God had promised this opportunity of a special spiritual childhood for many generations. Quoting the Old Testament prophet Samuel, he repeated the promise of God: ". . . And I will receive you, and will be a father unto you, and ye shall be my sons and daughters, saith the Lord Almighty" (2 Cor. 6:17–18, KJV).

Throughout the New Testament this promise is repeated. In Revelation 21:7, having described the awesome glories of the new heaven and new earth to come, the Scripture states, "He that overcometh shall inherit all things; and I will be his God, and *he shall be my son*" (RSV, emphasis mine).

These verses clearly refer to an experience of spiritual childhood which goes far beyond being merely a part of God's created universe. What is involved here is an intimacy with God reserved for those individuals who specifically seek it—an intimacy so rich and close that it is best described by using the model of a parent's love and care. God, having made us, loves us enough to adopt us as His children.

"Consider the incredible love that the Father has shown us in allowing us to be called 'children of God'—and that is not just what we are called, but what we *are*. Our heredity on the Godward side is no mere figure of speech. . . . Oh, dear children of mine . . . have you realized it? Here and now we *are* God's children" (1 John 3:1–2, Phillips).

The question, of course, is how to become God's children in that "incredible" sense of which John speaks.

3

Choosing to Be a
Child of God

"Do not be surprised because I tell you that
you must all be born again."
John 3:7, TEV

How can an adult, so accustomed to the role
and behaviors of maturity, become a child again?

Jesus was asked specifically that question by a
prominent Jewish leader named Nicodemus:
"'Rabbi, we know that you are a teacher sent by
God. No one could perform the miracles you are
doing unless God were with him.'

"Jesus answered, 'I am telling you the truth: no
one can see the Kingdom of God unless he is born
again.'

"'How can a grown man be born again?'
Nicodemus asked. 'He certainly cannot enter his
mother's womb and be born a second time!'

"'I am telling you the truth,' replied Jesus.
'that no one can enter the Kingdom of God unless

he is born of water and the Spirit. A person is born physically of human parents, but he is born spiritually of the Spirit. Do not be surprised because I tell you that you must all be born again. . . . I am telling you the truth: we speak of what we know and report what we have seen'" (John 3:2–11, TEV).

In the 1970s in the United States, the phrase, "born again," was so casually tossed around that it lost much of its impact. It became a buzz word used by journalists and popular writers to describe virtually every kind of conservative Christian practice. The phrase came to be something of a catchall socioreligious label, and many people have grown wary of using it in reference to themselves. Actually, the phrase "born again," as used in the Bible, is not a voguish way of categorizing one's overall lifestyle; it is a way of stating that a person has accepted a place in God's family. It means that an individual has chosen to be a child of God, and has made the first step in that direction.

This first step in becoming a child of God is the act of repentance—the single act of praying the sinner's prayer, confessing one's sins and asking that they be forgiven. Being born again, then, is not a state into which one gradually evolves. Sometimes individuals who grow up in the church, surrounded constantly by hymns and sermons and discussions of Christian life, can actually find themselves seeking to know God better without ever having taken this first critical step. Having a desire to understand God better, wanting to experience the personal intimacy with Him that they hear others talk about, such "cultural Christians" might sincerely seek ways to feel closer to God, never having engaged in that first, simple act of repentance. They are drawn by the attractiveness of being in the family of God, but somehow omit the process of being born into it!

"A journey of a thousand miles," says an old proverb, "begins with a single step." The pursuit of true spiritual childhood, the attempt to know God better by becoming more childlike in one's posture toward Him, makes sense only after one has become a part of the family. It is the promise of Scripture that one can achieve a richer discipleship through childlikeness, but the entire process must begin with forgiveness of sins and the new birth.

There are many ways to exercise one's spiritual childhood, many ways of optimizing the benefits of being God's son or daughter. The analogy of the natural parent-child relationship contains many lessons for us; it can teach us how best to play the role of God's child, in order to receive His richest blessings. But childhood always begins with birth, just as surely in the spiritual as in the natural order of things. Growing up in God's family starts with being born again—choosing to come to God in repentance and accept His forgiveness. Without that official act, all the rest is mere "head games," empty speculation, cheap psychology. That is what Christ was telling Nicodemus, just as He told many others: *the new birth is where spiritual life must always begin.*

Obviously, being born is just the beginning.

We cannot imagine the event of birth being all there is to life—nor even birth ushering us immediately into adulthood. A child is born, and for many years thereafter is still a child. Why do we expect a different process in the spiritual life?

God wants us, expects us, to be like children in certain aspects of our relationship with Him. He has so designed us. It is the natural mode by which God and man relate to one another, and when we neglect it, we miss an opportunity for emotional and spiritual intimacy with Him.

Though the life of every believer begins in the same way—with the new birth—some Christians are obviously more successful than others in reaching a satisfying experience with Him on a daily basis. Trying to find that way of feeling close to God and discovering how to have that sense of personal interaction with Him can be a major and sometimes frustrating challenge for a Christian. After my sins are forgiven, then what? How does He want to respond to me? How do I talk to Him—as to a partner? Or a pal? Or an authority figure? Or a stranger who has given me a gift? Or do I just leave Him alone until I need Him again, or wait for Him to get in touch with me?

What is the model for interacting with God?— that is the basic question. We need a pattern to follow, one which shows us how to address God. Part of the problem is that there are so many biblically based models available to us. Each contains its own truth about God, and its own lesson for us:

—We are soldiers in the army of God.
—We are laborers in God's vineyard.
—We are athletes, running a race for His approval.
—We are the bride, and He is the bridegroom.
—We are slaves, and He is our Master.

—God is our Judge. He is our High Priest. He
    is our King.

As a young Christian attending college, I was
fond of these stronger, more masculine metaphors,
and I tended to think in terms of them as I prayed
and thought about God. I was inclined particularly
toward the military analogy, as I suspect many
young men are. I always knelt to pray with the
sense of myself as a good soldier reporting to my
commanding officer. Stalwart. Brave. Ready for
duty. The martial sounds of "Onward Christian
Soldiers" were always faintly audible to me as I
thought about God. As I became a bit older and
began working in a church, I gravitated more
toward a "partner" image of my relationship with
God. I found the idea of being a colaborer with God
an appealing concept. He had lots of work to do and
I was out there alongside, doing my share.

But neither of these mental structures served
me well, over the long term, in developing a
workable sense of who God is and who I am in
relation to Him. My spiritual life began to lose
vitality. The fact of being a Christian was meaning
less and less to me. Real communication with God
in a close-up, personal way became more difficult,
and I therefore engaged in it less frequently. Life
began to beat me around a bit, as it will do, and I
needed to pray to someone other than a
Commanding Officer or a divine Co-worker. I was
still very much a Christian believer, but that
condition seemed to have less impact on the way I
felt about life in general. I didn't need a new God,
but I needed a fresh way of thinking about Him, of

talking to Him—a fresh mental and emotional posture toward Him.

When I found a "new" way of thinking about God, it was in fact an old and familiar one—but it rejuvenated my own personal walk with God, and that new-old version of God remains fresh and profound to me today. It is the conscious, determined effort to see God as my Father, to think of myself as a child, as His child, and to take seriously all the implications that flow from that metaphor. I understand that this is only one way of looking at God, but for me it has been the way which has made possible, for the first time in my life, a sense of genuine intimacy with a personal God.

Coming to God as a child is a state of mind, a posture which one voluntarily takes. It is a role which the Christian plays, a status he or she accepts. The believer must take the posture of the child in order for the emotional dynamics of the parent-child relationship to operate. God alone cannot produce those dynamics. Mere genetics do not make a parent-child relationship. The child must be willing to be the child before the parent can be the parent.

Can you imagine the difficulty of playing the role of a father to a grown child who refuses to interact except as a peer? It is easy for me to be "Dad" to Brian, my eight-year-old son. He still thinks of himself as my little boy; he still enjoys curling up in my lap; he wants me to kiss him goodnight and tuck him into bed. Being fatherly toward him comes easily, and I do it with great pleasure, because he is willing to be my little child.

But what if, in a few years, Brian feels too big and grown-up for all that, and refuses to engage in what he might regard then as childish behavior? It will be difficult for me to act as his father in the way I do now. I can only play parent to the degree that he plays child. He sets the tone. It is he who determines whether the psychological and emotional dynamics of the parent-child relationship will operate between us, or whether I will merely be his father in a genetic sense. For me to function as a father, he must be willing to function as a child.

Functioning as a child is not always easy for adults to do as they approach God. We spend a lifetime trying to grow up. We are urged to be self-reliant and mature, to grow beyond the dependencies and vulnerabilities of childhood. Being a self-sufficient adult is our goal for the first twenty years of life. We constantly push toward adulthood and independence. Then finally we arrive there, proud of our hard-earned competence and ability to stand on our own two feet, and we walk up to the recruiting table and offer to enlist in the army of God's Kingdom. And what does God tell us?

"Unless you change your whole outlook and become like little children you will never enter the kingdom of Heaven" (Matt. 18:3, Phillips).

That is not an easy role to accept in a world which places such a premium on skill and success and personal autonomy. Little wonder that people want to slide right past that verse and think instead of themselves as soldiers of the cross! But God understands the fact that, before we are ready for the battles of life, we must be His sons and daughters. He wants to love us as children. He knows we need the warmth and closeness that He can give us best as a caring Father, if we are willing to crawl into His lap and become His little children.

I have two daughters, both just reaching adolescence. I want them to grow up into successful, independent adults. I want them to achieve greatly, to become well-turned-out, thoroughly modern women. Whether they become lawyers or teachers or creative homemakers, I want them to be the very best. But when they have done all that, I still want them to come home to me and to call me "Daddy," and to be, in a certain sense, my little girls. If they get too big and too sophisticated and too independent to be my little girls, I will have lost them. And I will have lost my ability to be "Daddy" to them.

Likewise with God our Father. He sees us tackle the challenges of life, and He applauds our competence and skill, our ambition and energy. He is pleased by our emotional maturity and toughness. But He still wants to be father to us. He still wants us to come to Him as His little children, because He knows how much we need it.

4

Just Like a Child

"Unless you change your whole outlook
and become like little children you will never
enter the kingdom of Heaven."
Matthew 18:3, Phillips

It was the first time I ever experienced stage
fright.

I was a young boy about eight years old, sitting
with the other boys my age on the front pew of the
church during a revival service. The speaker was a
traveling evangelist, from South Africa as I recall.
That morning he paused in his sermon, scanned the
pew where we youngsters were sitting, and decided
he needed one of us to serve as a prop for the point
he was trying to make. He pointed his finger. I was
chosen. "Come to the platform," I heard him
saying. Nearly paralyzed with fear, I did as he said,
standing rigidly onstage beside him, in front of those
hundreds of people, as he used me to illustrate
some part of his message which I have long since
forgotten.

It was a fleeting and unimportant moment to everyone else in the church that day, but to me it was an unforgettable experience standing there, all eyes on me, with nothing to do but wish fervently to be somewhere—anywhere—else! I think of that church service every time I read the story in Matthew 18. I wonder if the child in the story was as scared as I was. I would like to think not. I would like to think Jesus somehow kept him from being that frightened:

"It was at this time that the disciples came to Jesus with the question, 'Who is really greatest in the kingdom of Heaven?' Jesus called a little child to his side and set him on his feet in the middle of them all. 'Believe me,' he said, 'unless you change your whole outlook and become like little children you will never enter the kingdom of Heaven. It is the man who can be as humble as this little child who is greatest in the kingdom of Heaven'" (vv. 2–4, Phillips).

Jesus obviously wished to answer the question that day in a way that His disciples would not soon forget. He not only *told* them; He *showed* them that entering the kingdom required that they become children again.

Christ's answer must have been a shock to His audience. The question they asked showed that being with Jesus had done little, up until then, to curb their naturally competitive instincts. They were essentially lining up to play the age-old game of "Who's on Top?" They wanted Jesus to tell them the rules of the game so they could keep score. "How can we know which one of us is top banana, Lord? Is it the best preacher, or the one who raises the most money, or the man who knows theology best? Is it the one of us who prays the most, or works the hardest, or brings out the biggest crowd to see you, Lord? Who's the greatest in the Kingdom, Lord?"

Imagine what a rebuke to their competitive spirit was the sight of that little child standing before them!

What did Jesus mean that day, challenging those mature, independent adults to be like little children? Compared to adults, children are relatively small, weak, emotionally erratic, intellectually undeveloped, dependent creatures. Certainly Christ was not advocating that those qualities be adopted by His disciples. But the dramatic way in which He answered the question leaves no doubt that He meant his answer to be taken seriously. There are clearly some important qualities of childhood which God wishes us to cultivate, however old and mature we become.

Quality #1: Children have a simple, sometimes naïve faith in the ability of the parent to do good things for them.

My daughter Vanessa once was given a helium-filled balloon at Sunday school. It was bright blue, and to a two-year-old it must have seemed almost alive as it danced and floated on the end of a string. She was intrigued by her new toy, and she ran through the halls of the church that day pulling it along behind her, watching it bob brightly in the air above her head.

But the inevitable happened. The balloon finally bumped into the sharp edge of a metal railing and popped. With a single, loud "bang," it burst and fell to her feet. She looked down and saw at the end of the string not a marvelous, bouncing, nearly-alive balloon, but a forlorn wad of wet blue rubber. The sudden transformation seemed to startle her, but only briefly. She paused for only a second, then happily picked up the shredded rubber, marched cheerfully to where I was standing, and thrust it up at me.

"Here, Daddy," she chirped confidently, "fix it!"

We adults have a way of making a mess of things at times. We don't always know how to avoid trouble; we seem almost to invite it. We can take the bright promise of our youth and somehow squander it. We can begin a marriage with the best of intentions on both sides and convert it into bitter separation and divorce. We ruin good friendships with carelessness or neglect. We set goals and resolutions and fail to follow through.

Or sometimes bad things just happen. Sometimes we see the happy circumstances of our lives, through no fault of our own, burst into sorrow. Suddenly the gaily bouncing balloon is a miserable heap of rubber.

Such times are times for childlike confidence in the ability of the Father to "fix it." Like the two-year-old, we bring our messed-up lives, our ruptured plans, our broken relationships, our wet handfuls of burst balloon, and we offer them to a Father whom we trust to make it right. Without questioning, without analyzing the apparent difficulty of the task, we simply realize that *this* problem is too big for us to solve, and we offer it to the Father for His intervention. We know He *can* fix it, and we believe He *will*.

Many examples of this childlike faith occurred in the life of Christ, and He almost always rewarded it.

Leprosy was probably the most devastating disease which afflicted people in Christ's culture. It was considered impossible even to treat, much less to cure, leprosy; contracting the disease was not only a certain death sentence, but a guarantee of being forced to live as a shadowy outcast until one died. Leprosy was considered a loathsome, untouchable condition, and one didn't even think in terms of recovering from it. Only a child would be naïve enough to expect to be cured of leprosy.

But one leper, described by Matthew, had that kind of naïve expectation. "And now a leper approached him, bowed low, and said, 'Sir, if only you will, you can cleanse me.' Jesus stretched out his hand, touched him, and said, 'Indeed I will; be clean again.' And his leprosy was cured immediately" (Matt. 8:1–3, NEB).

Just like a child.

On a different occasion, a woman who had suffered from a blood disease for many years somehow had the naïve, childish idea that simply by touching Jesus' clothes she would get better. Jesus was in the region where she lived, and she decided to seek physical recovery in this childlike way. "Jesus [went on,] accompanied by a great crowd which pressed upon him. Among them was a woman who had suffered from haemorrhages for twelve

years; and in spite of long treatment by many
doctors, on which she had spent all she had, there
had been no improvement; on the contrary, she had
grown worse. She had heard what people were
saying about Jesus, so she came up from behind in
the crowd and touched his cloak; for she said to
herself, 'If I touch even his clothes, I shall be
cured.'

"And there and then the source of her
haemorrhages dried up and she knew in herself that
she was cured of her trouble. At the same time
Jesus, aware that power had gone out of Him,
turned round in the crowd and asked, 'Who touched
me?' . . . He was looking round to see who had
done it. And the woman, trembling with fear when
she grasped what had happened to her, came and
fell at his feet and told Him the whole truth. He
said to her, 'My daughter, your faith has cured
you. . . .'" (Mark 5:24–34, NEB).

Just like a child.

Impulsively trusting Him to do what none of
her doctors had done, this woman offered to Him
her seemingly unfixable problem, and He fixed it. It
is interesting that three different writers tell this
story in the Gospels, and that, while each tell it a
bit differently, all three writers mention that Christ,
when He spoke to the woman, called her
"daughter"! She came to Him as His little child, and
that led Him to play the role of Father. She was so
childlike that He could only be fatherly in response.

Just Like a Child

Quality #2: Children have the capacity for being dazzled and awestruck by the wonders of the world around them.

There were twelve of us children in the Conn household when I was growing up, and there was rarely enough money for glamorous vacation trips and entertainment. My father, however, was one of the all-time great excitement-mongers I have ever known. He knew how to make the most mundane activities seem adventuresome. He was a natural hype-artist, a born razzle-dazzler, and he used those talents to make life constantly exciting for his twelve children. When he did find the money to take us on a trip, he primed us for the event so thoroughly that it usually assumed enormous proportions in our young minds.

On one such occasion, Dad took three of us boys to Washington, D.C. In the weeks preceding the trip, Dad bombarded us with stories of Washington, books about Washington, photographs of Washington. We dug into the encyclopedias and old issues of *National Geographic*. We virtually memorized the details of all the famous buildings and monuments in the capital city. Dad had us so well prepared, so eager to actually be there, that by the time our old Buick finally rolled north through Virginia and into the city of Washington I was almost too excited to sit still in the back seat.

We drove slowly through the city, taking it all in. As we passed each of the famous landmarks, so familiar from all the pre-trip buildup, I shouted in high-pitched, childish excitement, "Hey, look, there's the Washington Monument! I've heard of that all my life!" We turned a corner. "Hey! Wow! There's the White House! I've heard of that all my life!" Up the street I would spot another familiar sight and yell at my brothers to look: "Hey, look, fellas, the Capitol building! I've heard of that all my life!"

Finally my brother, Phil, three years older and weary of my childish, awestruck outbursts, spoke up with a tone of weary sophistication. We turned a corner, passing an ordinary-looking service station, and he pointed a finger out the window and declared drily, "Wow, look, fellas, there's a Shell Oil station. I've heard of *that* all my life!"

How quickly the wide-eyed child becomes the jaded and somewhat cynical adolescent! Young children have an endless capacity for awe, for wonder—a willingness to be amazed and dazzled. As we get older, we lose that quality. We come to the point that we have seen it all, heard it all, done it all before, and "Wow!" fades into "ho-hum." A child can be entertained and impressed by the sight of a bug crawling across the sidewalk, while his adult counterpart remains bored in the face of all sorts of miracles occurring virtually before his eyes.

I have often seen a congregation of adult Christians stand and recite the Apostles' Creed with all the excitement of a slowly dripping faucet. Sometimes I am one of them. I hear myself repeating the familiar words of a hymn, hear the monotony in my voice, and realize that I am speaking or singing of great miracles, of the person of God living in my heart, of the death of a Man being punished for my crimes! And I ask myself, "How can I speak of such exciting things with so little excitement?!" The words and the emotion do not match. I find myself singing, with detached preoccupation, of things which ought to dazzle and humble me.

One of the qualities of childhood which I believe God will help us recapture is the capacity to be awestruck, to be smitten with a sense of wonder at the great things God has done for us. We need to become, from time to time, like the country boy at the fair, our minds newly boggled at the miracles of God. "I stand amazed in the presence/Of Jesus the Nazarene," the old hymn goes, "And wonder how He could love me,/A sinner, condemned, unclean./How marvelous! How wonderful! And my song will ever be;/How marvelous! How wonderful! Is my Savior's love for me!"

This need for a childlike sense of awe at God's greatness is especially critical for Christians who have been in the church for many years. It is an axiom that familiarity breeds contempt, and that process is as true in religious life as in any other area. After so many years of singing the same songs, hearing the same sermons and stories, and praying the same prayers, it is difficult to retain the freshness one felt at the start. There is some evidence that even Christ's original twelve disciples had this problem of gradually taking more and more for granted the special qualities of the Master who at first meeting had so overwhelmed each of them.

As we feel this quite natural process setting in, we must pray a specific prayer for God to restore in us the childlike eyes with which to see Him again. It is a prayer which He will answer: "Give me a child's eyes, Lord, to be dazzled and thunderstruck by the wonder of your love. Reduce me, Lord, to an innocent, open-mouthed child again."

Quality #3: Children can imagine the future, even when it bears little resemblance to the present.

Once in Boston I took my children to see an Ice Capades show in which the star skater was Olympic gold medalist Dorothy Hamill. The show was a bright and glamorous one, with swirling spotlights and spectacular costumes, and we were all captivated by the grace and beauty of the skaters.

A day or so later, sitting in our apartment, I looked up from the newspaper I was reading to see six-year-old Heather gliding across the living-room floor. She was dressed in one of her mother's pastel-colored slips, the straps wrapped carefully around her head, and she shuffled across the carpeted floor with a lurching stride. "What in the world are you doing?!" I demanded in bewilderment. She paused to give me a puzzled look, as if I had asked an exceptionally stupid question, and answered without missing a beat, "I'm winning the gold medal at the Winter Olympics!" And with that she skated, in her beat-up little sneakers, into the next room.

Every parent has a similar memory of a time when a child has been absorbed with her own private vision of the future. To children, drawn so powerfully by the fantasies of what they might become, the present sometimes doesn't really matter. The future is so real that it can be simply wallowed in, without self-consciousness or worry about how different it is from present reality. A little boy can put on a football helmet and a pair of shoulder pads, stand in front of a bathroom mirror, squint a bit, and almost *be* Mean Joe Greene. He doesn't see a seventy-pound third-grader with several teeth missing and very little meat on the bones; he sees a mean, lean, football-playing machine! He sees a mobile, agile, hostile linebacker or fullback or whatever his latest gridiron fantasy might be. A little girl can put on her mother's hat and fur wrap, stare into a mirror, look right past the freckles and snaggly teeth, and see the beautiful woman she will one day become.

That childish ability to imagine tomorrow, unbothered by today's reality, is a characteristic which can be a valuable part of every Christian's attitude toward ourselves and what God is making of us. God has always been in the business of reconstructing lives. He has always looked at people not for what they are, but for what they can become with His help. He has no trouble looking past the flaws and weaknesses of the present and seeing what we are going to be tomorrow. But we do have trouble doing that! We are too aware of how we are today, too preoccupied with the mess we are currently in, to see where God is taking us.

"Become like this little child," Jesus said. Learn to squint just a bit and see the new "you" God is making, and try not to be dismayed by the flaws in the current version.

Remember the woman Christ met at the well, the Samaritan woman who had five ex-husbands and one live-in boyfriend? She was so intimidated by her shabby reputation in the little town of Sychar that she came to fill her waterpot at a time calculated to avoid the neighbors. But when she met Christ she quit hiding from the townspeople, and instead immediately sought them out, aggressively spreading to them the word of the Messiah. She obviously accepted herself as new, as reborn—a worthy person because Christ had made her so.

Jesus could look at the frightened, vacillating Peter and see the bold leader of the apostolic church. Jesus could look at the cautious, doubting Thomas and see the man who would eventually offer his own life as ultimate proof of his faith. Jesus could look at the disgraced, fallen woman named Mary Magdalene and see the virtuous believer she was in the process of becoming. He looked at the rebellious youth named Augustine and saw the future saint. He looked at an indecisive monk named Martin Luther and saw the great Reformer. He looked at a strung-out, disintegrating country singer named Johnny Cash and saw a great witness. He looked at an arrogant, deceitful lawyer named Chuck Colson and saw a committed spiritual leader.

He looks at you and me as we approach Him, tentatively, not knowing how we can ever measure up to the demands of discipleship, and He sees the transformed children of God He plans to make of us. The difficulty we have is to get *us* to see it. We are too hooked on what we are now, how we feel now, how far we have to go, to see ourselves as He sees us. He wants us, like the freckled-faced girl or the skinny little boy at the mirror, to look past the child of today and see tomorrow's beautiful grownup.

Quality #4: The child, being willing to listen to instruction, is easily taught.

My wife and I took up the sport of downhill skiing at the ripe old age of thirty-four years.

Just Like a Child

I grew up in the Deep South, where skiing on snow was considered a peculiar form of insanity practiced by Yankees and Europeans. But my brother—one who had led me into other types of athletic mischief—induced me to try the sport, and at a relatively advanced age I found myself standing at the top of a snow-covered hill with a pair of long, slick boards strapped to my feet.

Over the next few weeks, I learned to do something which resembled skiing—and which did, in fact, get me from the top of the hill to the bottom with a minimum of bodily damage. But it didn't come easily. My progress was slow and awkward. I fell frequently, from time to time entertaining, with a truly spectacular wipe-out, those who watched. I was scared most of the time. I ate lots of snow on a strictly involuntary basis. But eventually I did learn to ski; and after two years of slow but steady improvement I had been so badly bitten by the skiing bug that I was eager for my three children to take up the sport.

Their time to learn came at the ages of seven, ten, and twelve. We took them to a small ski hill near Boston, where we lived that winter, rented their equipment, and enrolled them in a beginners' class. I sent them to that first ski class feeling much like Chinese mothers must have felt when they bound their babies' feet; this will be a slow, painful process, I thought, but worth it in the end. I remembered my own clumsy start, and felt almost guilty for sending my children through such an ordeal.

As one might guess, it didn't work out that way at all. By the end of the first day, my children were

moving comfortably on their skis. After two days
they were making smooth turns down the easy
slopes. The third day they were riding the lifts to
the top of the mountain to ski with their mother and
me. And by the end of the second week, I was
shouting to them to wait for us older folks as they
zipped down the mountain ahead of us! Within two
weeks, they learned to ski almost as well as we had
learned in two years.

In discussing my children's experience with
other parents and with their ski instructors, I found
that the pattern in our family was a common one. It
is virtually a cliché in the sport: children learn faster
and more naturally than adults. They are less afraid,
enjoy the process more, and don't seem to mind
falling and getting up again quite so much as adults.
They absorb instructions more readily, and have
fewer of those counterproductive ways of doing
things to eliminate so that the correct movements
can be learned. They are less likely to devise their
own homemade strategies for getting from point A
to point B, and therefore they learn to do it the
instructor's way from the start.

As adults, we all have developed our own
individual strategies for dealing with life. Sometimes
they work, sometimes they don't, but they are *our*
strategies, and we tend to cling to them. God has
much to teach us, but to learn His lessons we must
sometimes abandon our own ways of doing things
and trust His instruction. That requires a certain
humility which doesn't come easily. Taking pride, as
we do, in our ability to cope, to fend for ourselves,
to make our way in life, we can find it difficult to

admit to ourselves that we haven't put all the pieces together properly.

The man in the Bible whom we call the "rich young ruler" apparently faced—and flunked—this particular test of childhood. He came to Jesus and described his strategy for finding eternal life.

"Here's how I'm going about it, Sir," he said, in effect. "Now tell me what else I have to do." And Jesus told him he had to abandon that entire approach of good works and self-sufficiency and become a schoolboy again in the school of God, to sit at the feet of the Master like a child and learn about the kingdom right from the beginning. It was that humbling descent into childhood which the young man apparently could not accept, and the Bible says he "went away sorrowful" (Mark 10:22, RSV).

God wants us to do it His way. He wants us to learn from Him—by reading His scriptures and seeking, in prayer, His insights—how to construct a balanced life. He wants us to try to put aside all our own preconceived notions and accept His teaching as the only way to do it.

Just like a child.

5
What Kind of Parent Is God?

"You saw how the Lord your God carried you, just
as a man carries his son."
Deuteronomy 1:31, NAS

If we can become children—with the qualities
of trust, awe, creative imagination, and an eagerness
to learn—what kind of Parent can we expect God to
be?

The most obvious answer is that God will do for
us, in a spiritual sense, all the things that a good
father does for his children in a natural relationship.
A good earthly father fills many diverse needs in the
lives of his children, but most of them can be
clustered into three major functions: (1) He sees that
the child's need fo.· protection and material things
are met; (2) He offers the child constant love and
personal contact; (3) He provides discipline and
teaching as the child grows up.

First, let's look at the role of God the Father in

meeting our needs for material things. Jesus painted
a beautiful picture in addressing this point in the
Sermon on the Mount: "Look at the birds flying
around," He said to His disciples. (I like to imagine
they literally did that, in that outdoor setting, as He
talked of birds and flowers.) "[Birds] do not plant
seeds, gather a harvest and put it in barns; yet your
Father in heaven takes care of them! Aren't you
worth much more than birds? Can any of you live a
bit longer by worrying about it? And why worry
about clothes? Look how the wild flowers grow: they
do not work or make clothes for themselves. But I
tell you that not even King Solomon with all his
wealth had clothes as beautiful as one of these
flowers. It is God who clothes the wild grass. . . .
Won't He be all the more sure to clothe you? . . .
So do not start worrying: 'Where will my food come
from? or my drink? or my clothes?' . . . Your Father
in heaven knows that you need all these things"
(Matt. 6:26–32, TEV).

Taken literally, that seems too good to be true.
It almost strains credibility to believe that the great
God Almighty, the Old-Testament Jehovah, He of
the thunderbolts and the terrible swift sword, looks
down at me and, when He sees me, feels all the
impulses of love and tenderness that I feel when I
look down at my own small child!

Unfortunately, the God many of us heard about
as youngsters in Sunday school was often described
as nine parts wrath to one part mercy. All the
visions from childhood of an angry, powerful God,
easily outraged and quick to punish—those visions
are still too alive deep inside for us to immediately
accept this fatherly God. Having grown up with
such an intimidating vision of God, we are reluctant

to trust this gentler version. *Is it really true, we wonder, that God's attitude toward us is best illustrated by our own attitude as parents toward our own children? Can that view of God be trusted, or is it merely wishful thinking?*

Jesus answered that question quite directly a little later in the same sermon: "Would any of you who are fathers give your son a stone when he asks for bread? Or would you give him a snake when he asks for a fish? As bad as you are, you know how to give good things to your children. How much more, then, will your Father in heaven give good things to those who ask him!" (Matt. 7:9–11, TEV).

That statement is an outright challenge to us to consider the parallels between our parental instincts and God's attitude toward us.

Does God want you to prosper? Does He care about your success in secular pursuits? Is it important to Him that you be happy in the fullest and best sense of that word?

The Matthew text is a good starting place for the answers to those questions. Jesus often taught, as He does here in the Sermon on the Mount, by asking questions. His disciples asked a question, and Jesus answered with a question of His own that showed them the truth. Our questions about success might also be answered that way.

Does it matter to *you* that *your* own child achieves and excels? Do you want to see that child succeed in school or sports or music? Do you take pleasure in his or her happiness?

Even in the areas of their lives which do not directly involve you, does it please you to see your children earn the rewards of their own hard work?

Of course it does! And so, also, we can be

confident that our Heavenly Father wishes the best
for us—not just in spiritual matters, but in every
part of our lives. "If you . . . quite naturally give
good things to your children, how much more likely
is it that your Heavenly Father will give good things
to those who ask him?"

There are limits, of course, to God's willingness
for us to have whatever we want. It would be
unreasonable to assume that God applauds every
goal we set. He does not always respond
approvingly as we charge toward those things we
want for ourselves, just as we don't desire for our
children everything they would like. Only an
indulgent and foolish father would take such an
uncritical approach to his children's pursuits.

We have all seen examples of such parental
pushovers and understand that they generally
produce spoiled and unhappy children. If we
recognize that it is no favor to a child to satisfy
indiscriminately all his or her wishes, then surely
our Heavenly Father recognizes this truth also!

I once heard a Christian say, speaking of a
personal goal in his life, "God knows how badly I
want this, and I know He wants me to be happy, so
it must be His will for me to have it." That is not a
reasonable conclusion—certainly not if we use the
Matthew text as our guide—but it frequently
appears, directly or indirectly, in the attitudes of
high-achieving, ambitious Christians.

God may have very good reasons for
withholding certain things from us, things we
greatly desire, things for which we have worked
hard, things we think we absolutely can't live
without.

What Kind of Parent Is God?

Part of being God's child is accepting those reasons. It goes with the territory. We are His children, and as surely as that brings good gifts from Him, it also requires bowing to His better judgment about things. The important point is that the ultimate outcomes are always good. *Always.*

Even in secular matters. God is our Heavenly Father even in the areas of our lives that seem totally nonspiritual. Some people have trouble believing that. They have God locked up in the church, pasted up on the stained-glass window, maybe chained to a pew somehow, so that He is master of what goes on inside the sanctuary but is uninterested in whatever goes on outside.

We have no difficulty believing that God cares about the sins we commit, the tithes and offerings we pay, the church we attend, the prayers we pray, the Scripture we read or neglect to read. We all agree that He is interested in *those* things. But does it really matter to Him about the other stuff—the ordinary, run-of-the-mill stuff?

Does God care if you get that promotion? Catch that plane? Make that sale? Or if the interest rates go up too fast for you to buy that new house you've set your heart on? Does He really care if you make a "B" instead of a "C" in the classroom? Or if you hit the ball out-of-bounds off the tee? Or if the dinner gets done before the guests arrive? Or whether your hair looks good tonight?

Does it matter to Him whether you make a little money or a lot of money, whether you win first prize or second, whether you get a date to the senior prom? Is God—the one, true, only, all-powerful Jehovah God—really so fatherly that He cares about such trivial matters in the lives of ordinary people?

Yes! Emphatically, absolutely, miraculously, the answer is yes! It *does* matter. Not just the supernatural things, but the natural things, matter to Him.

Jesus cared about the little things in the lives of those He encountered. He cared whether His mother's friend had enough wine for her wedding guests. Cared so much, in fact, that He *did* something about it. He made more wine. Nothing particularly spiritual about that. In some ways, turning water to wine was the most revealing miracle Jesus ever performed, because it demonstrated that His interest and concern extend beyond the forgiving of sin and the healing of disease. The little things mattered to Jesus.

It mattered that His disciples were seasick and scared to death, so He calmed the storm. It mattered that the people who came to see Him became hungry, so He manufactured food right on the spot. It mattered that His friends Martha and Mary grieved over the death of their brother— mattered so much, in fact, that He wept right along with them, even though He undoubtedly knew that in a few minutes their grief would be ended. Jesus wept with them, because their grief mattered to Him.

The foundation of a happy life is the knowledge that we matter to God. We are His children, and He wants good things for us, even to the point of becoming actively involved in the everyday affairs of our lives.

In life's little daily challenges, God is not

neutral; He is actively on your side. He is on your side in those constant battles with the "blahs," and the family budget, and the crabgrass in the lawn. He is involved with you in your struggles with that smoking habit you can't seem to whip, and the bad plumbing upstairs, and all those other things that get you down.

He cares.

He cares because you are His child.

On the other hand . . .

However badly we may want certain things from life, and however willing God is for us to live richly and fully, a Christian cannot expect to sail through life getting whatever his heart desires.

Consider these three situations in which a parent might say "no" to a child, or in which our Heavenly Father might not assist us in achieving or experiencing those things we have wanted for ourselves.

1. *God may not help us have what we desire if it involves rebellion against Him or rejection of Him.* Would you help your child run away from home? Or give him the money to do something in direct defiance of your orders? Not likely. Nor is God likely to help us reach goals that constitute willful movement away from Him. However much He wants us to be happy, He wants us, first of all, to be His. When we rebel against Him and consciously violate His will for us as we know it, He can no longer be expected to help us get where we want to go.

Rebellion of this sort may take different forms. It may involve breaking God's moral code, breaking His law. Or it may be a more personal type of rebellion, an act of ours that involves disobedience of what we know, in our hearts, God has called us to do. This is a highly subjective, intensely personal experience. No one can make a judgment in this area but the Christian disciple himself.

A biblical example of this type of rebellion is found in the story of Jonah. God told him to go to Nineveh to preach, and Jonah flatly refused to go. He had other plans. It doesn't appear that he sinned or broke God's moral law in any flagrant way, except that he had a clear sense that God wanted him to do one thing, and he set out to do something else instead. So God, rather than facilitating his plans, frustrated them, and that's why Jonah ultimately found himself in the belly of a whale.

There is no reason to believe that God has stopped interacting with people in this way. He still has specific things for specific people to do at specific times. When He does, that person will always know. The individual may perceive it as a calling, or a divine inspiration to do a certain thing, or as some other private experience that may take a variety of forms. Only God and the person involved can know for sure. But when that sense of needing to obey God is there and we ignore it or rebel against it, God cannot then be expected to assist us as we go in our own direction.

2. *God may not help us reach our goals if we don't select them in consultation with Him.* God expects us to submit our plans to Him. He wants us to talk to Him about our plans—not after the fact,

but all along the way. As parents, we dislike having full-blown plans dropped into our laps, already neatly packaged and set in motion by our children. (Even less do we like to find out what our kids are doing *after* they've botched things for themselves.) We like to be consulted as they go along, and to have opportunity for input as their plans and goals are developing.

So does God. The Book of Proverbs is scattered with expressions of the idea that God wants to be involved in the daily process, not just to have things announced to Him on rare occasions—like on Easter Sunday or when we're in big trouble! "In all thy ways acknowledge him, and he shall direct thy paths" (Prov. 3:6, KJV). The word *acknowledge* is the interesting one in this familiar verse; it is such a gentle word, such a carefully chosen word, urging the child of God to allow God into his planning. God doesn't want to take over our lives, to call the shots, to jerk us into line and make us do things in a particular way. "Acknowledge him," the verse says. Just acknowledge Him; just give Him a chance to provide some direction.

In another place, we read the same call for interaction with God at the goal-setting stage: "Commit to the Lord whatever you do, and your plans will succeed" (Prov. 16:3, NIV).

Whatever you do. The Bible is clearly not talking just to preachers here. This verse does not refer to the high and lofty things of the church, the sacred things of the priesthood. This is a call to the everyday believer, to the simplest child of God— both a call and a promise to the businessman and the housewife-mother, to the student in the library and the schoolteacher who feels like giving up. To all of us it is both a challenge and a promise: "Commit it to God, and He will help it to succeed."

It is particularly interesting that this verse talks about *plans*. It is the *plans* that God wants to take a look at. Not the past. Not the already-squandered days. Not even the things that are now in progress. God wants us to commit the *plans* to Him—the *goals*, the dreams, the things out there in the future that draw you so powerfully that you're willing to write them down on a piece of paper and dream about them and work toward them. Those are the things God will help to succeed, but He wants to be involved while the plans are being formed, not after things are already underway.

3. *God may not help us reach our goals if reaching them will ultimately bring us pain.* As natural parents, we so often tell our children no, on the basis of our superior wisdom, that the catch phrase, "father knows best," has become part of the vocabulary. When all else fails, when we are unable to talk our children out of something we don't want them to have, we always resort to the old standby, "No, son, I know you're too young to understand it, but this wouldn't be good for you. I realize how badly you want it, but I know what's best for you."

We've all heard that speech—or given it—a hundred times. But of course the parents' "superior" wisdom sometimes isn't superior at all. The parent, like the child, is often just guessing, and he is often wrong.

That is not the case with God. He knows the end from the beginning. He knows every turn in the path, every square inch of the landscape, every nook and cranny of a great big world we are just beginning to discover. This Father *does* know best— every time—and He wouldn't be a loving Father if He allowed us to have things He knows will be ultimately destructive.

Would you give your small child a loaded revolver to play with, or a sharp knife? Would you give your child a wolf for a playmate, even if the child found the wolf cute and cuddly and saw no danger? Of course not. And neither will God, if we commit our plans to Him, allow us things that will destroy us. No matter how much we reach for them, He will protect us from our own mistakes.

There is another time God may say no to our goals, and that is *when we are not yet ready for the thing we seek.* Would you let your son borrow the family car at the age of ten? Or let your daughter go to grownup movies when she's still in grade school? You would refuse them, even if you felt there was nothing intrinsically wrong with what they wanted to do. You may allow your son or daughter all those things in due time, but you'll say no for now, because you know your child just isn't ready for them yet.

God's timing is always better than ours. He brings us along slowly and skillfully. But we are impatient; we want it all now. Sometimes we set goals that may be good goals, worthy goals, but which we are not ready to handle. When we do, it only makes sense that a loving Father will keep those things out of our reach.

Only God knows what might be the implication for your overall well-being if you become famous or wealthy—or if you married that girl, got that promotion, or simply could afford to move to that neighborhood in which you've always wanted to live. He knows.

And part of what it means to be God's children is to accept that He knows, and that He will bring what is best into our lives—not what we want every time, but what is ultimately best for us.

6

FatherCare—and
MotherCare

"Just as a father loves his children, so the
Lord loves those who fear Him."
Psalm 103:13, Beck

Every father understands that it is his duty to
put food on the table and clothing on the backs of
his little children. To provide such basic material
needs is universally agreed to be the irreducible
minimum in a father's responsibility.

The best fathers, however, realize that the job
of providing for their children has just begun when
the groceries are bought and the rent is paid. The
best fathers also provide love, a special brand of
masculine love that only a father can give. For a
father who is deeply involved in his role as provider
and breadwinner, taking the time to make direct
expressions of love and affection for his child can
seem unnecessary or even awkward. "I work hard
all day to provide for my family, and that is my

expression of love," reasons the father. But that is not good enough. The father's responsibility does not end when he has put food on the table. A good father also shows his children love through direct expressions of affection.

God, similarly, does not invest all his fatherliness in His promise to supply our material needs; He is also our source of parental love and nurture.

Lee Salk, a well-known psychiatrist, recently wrote a book titled *My Father, My Son,* in which he interviews scores of young men about their relationships with their fathers, and draws some conclusions based on these interviews. One of the most interesting sections in this fascinating book is Salk's explanation of the need so many boys and men express for a more loving, caring father. Over and over, the interviewees describe respect and admiration for their fathers, but also regret that there had not been more overt expressions of love between them. "Not one male interviewed," reports Salk, "wished his father had been less demonstrative. No one said, 'My father was demonstrative, but I won't be that way with *my* son.'"

Salk summarizes this commonly expressed desire for closer contact with our fathers by referring to his own experience: "Caring is one thing. I mean, my father cared more about us than anything in the world, but he cared from afar. What matters is to be there on a daily basis. . . . I believe the most important thing about a father is his love—expressed in a real sense. Not just saying, 'Hey, I love you,' and letting it go at that. The most important thing in *our* relationship were those talks we had . . . after I got to know him and we had shed a few tears and had dropped all our defenses and our retention of emotions, and could look eye to eye, man to man, and say, 'I love you.'"

I once asked my students at Lee College to describe for me the single best memory they had of their fathers. Whether the event occurred ten years earlier, or a year, or a week, I instructed them to select the single slice of memory by which they most fondly remembered their fathers.

The responses were predictably varied, but probably the commonest memories were those in which the child and father had shared a *small* moment—memories in which the dominant theme was simply being together, doing something of no particular importance, but doing it together. Here are some examples:

● *"When he came home from work and he pulled me into his arms then put me on his shoulders. I felt so loved."*

● *"My dad taking the family camping and he always tended to the fire made to keep warm in the evening. He always took charge when we were in the mountains."*

● *"The best memory I have had with my father was the day we played a game of chase in the back yard when I was about seven years old."*

● *"My father and I used to go fishing a lot and I would steer the boat while he fished. The type of fishing we did was done at dusk and on into the early night. He sat in the front of the boat with a twenty-foot cane pole, which had bait on a hook hanging about twelve inches down, and he would slap the water with the end of the pole (jigger fishing). I remember those fishing trips."*

My own answer to the same question—"What is your single most positive memory of your father?"—is consistent with the pattern seen in these students' memories. I have shared many good times with my father, not only when I was a youngster, but in adulthood as well. I have lived near him, and have worked professionally with him, for most of my life, and enjoy hundreds of pleasant memories of him as a father. But when asked to recall a single memory which stands out as the warmest and best, I find myself remembering a particular moment from more than twenty-five years ago.

I was a boy, not even a teenager. Two of my brothers and I had accompanied Dad on a trip to some place in the Deep South. We were returning to our home in Tennessee late one night, driving the roomy old Buick. It was past midnight. I remember the darkness outside the car, the headlights probing the black road ahead as we pushed through the night.

My brothers had fallen asleep on the back seat; I alone remained awake with Dad in the front. I remember feeling that he was pleased that I was still awake to keep him company, and the sense of his unspoken welcome made me feel important to him. We rarely spoke. Occasionally there was a comment from one to the other, but no great intimacies were shared, not even a casual conversation. We were just *there together*, sitting in the dark; and to me the feeling of privacy and warmth, being with Dad with no competition for his attention, in no hurry to move on to anything else, was a delicious sensation that still resonates in my memory after all these years.

With children, there is sometimes no substitute for parental time—periods of unhurried, undivided attention. Often even the best parents forget that need, or develop lifestyles which provide no room for it. We find ourselves so problem-oriented as parents that we spend most of our time with our children as troubleshooters. When our child needs our help, whether to tie his shoes or to get a driver's license, we address the problem, help as best we can, and move on. But often there is no particular thing our children need from us; what they need is just for us to be there.

A friend told me of a time when his daughter stepped quietly into his study as he worked at his desk. Looking up as the child entered, he asked her, "What can I do for you, sweetheart?"

"Nothing," she replied timidly, as though unprepared for the question. "I just want to be where you are."

He realized, as she answered, how much like a *client* he had treated her. She appeared at his door, and he immediately thought of her in terms of something to be done, a small domestic problem to be solved, a "daughter-client" to be served. He moved instinctively to *do* for her, when all she wanted was for him to *be there*.

As God's children, we need to reach for those times spent with Him *just being together*. With God, however, the problem is never one of the availability of the Father to the child, but of the child's taking time to spend with the Father. God as a loving Parent is always there and always available for intimate contact, but we as His children must initiate the exchange.

The presence of God is a constant, real thing. Only our awareness of it, and our response to it, varies. David poetically describes the pervasive, inescapable presence of God in one of the most familiar Psalms:

Whither shall I go from thy Spirit?
   Or whither shall I flee from thy presence?
If I ascend to heaven, thou art there!
   If I make my bed in Sheol, thou art there!
If I take the wings of the morning
   and dwell in the uttermost parts of the sea,
even there thy hand shall lead me . . .
(Ps. 139:7–10, RSV)

The constant presence of God does not automatically guarantee healthy intimacy with Him, though. In fact, quite the opposite effect can result if we are taught always to "fear" the Lord, to be aware of His constant, brooding presence, but never to establish contact with Him as a Father.

Lee Salk, speaking of fatherhood in a natural sense, observes, "One of the most malignant elements in the father-son relationship is *proximity without communication.*" That the old man is always around, that he is always watching, can be an oppressive experience, rather than a supportive one, if there is never any positive, loving conversation between the child and him. The presence of our father becomes a positive part of our lives only if we are interacting with him in a loving way. Otherwise, he is, at best, a piece of furniture, or at worst, a bothersome watchdog.

That is true in the spiritual sense, as well. The problem with most individuals reared in the church is *not* that we are insufficiently impressed with the unrelenting presence of God. The problem is that we are not sufficiently taught how to experience His presence as that of a loving Father. There is between us and God an adequate sense of proximity, but an inadequate communication, and the result is indeed malignant. I remember hearing, as a child, the famous lines of Psalm 139 and being frightened rather than reassured by them. I experienced God's omnipresence then as "inescapable," rather than as "consistently reliable," which is the weight of that psalm to me today. The difference is not in God, of course, but in my ability to experience His fatherliness.

Just as we must ask the Father for what we need of a material nature, our need for His fatherly love will also be met only at our initiative. Unlike many earthly fathers, He is as much a giver of love as He is the provider of the tangible necessities of life. "Just as a father loves his children," says the psalmist, "so does God love those who fear Him."

A heavenly Mother?

Some fathers have difficulty showing their children the warmth and love they feel. Their love is deep and genuine, but they are awkward in expressing it overtly, and consequently don't try very often. Such fathers show their love by working hard and providing for the family, rather than expressing it in more personal ways. Touching and kissing and saying "I love you" are not what real love is all about, they reason; supporting the needs of one's family is what a father's love is all about.

That is a common view of fatherhood, and the problem with it is that it is only half right. The truth is that children *need* the touching and kissing and saying "I love you." They need it, in fact, maybe as much as they need shelter and a hot meal at night. The home which lacks continual expressions of warmth and personal affection is an impoverished home, just as surely as if there were no bread on the table or no heat in the furnace.

God realizes that, of course, so He created mothers!

For whatever cultural or biological reasons, mothers have a special touch, a special warmth that fathers often lack in communicating personal love for their children. Simple gestures of affection, stroking and touching, a sense of acceptance and concern—in short, all those qualities which add up to warm, nuturant parenthood—often seem to come more easily to mothers than to fathers and, consequently, are left to mothers in millions of homes. Christopher Leach, a British writer and father, described the special communication between mother and child in a particularly poignant way: "Children come from *within* the mother. A man shares; but he cannot truly know."

So father wins the bread and provides the discipline, while the mother nurtures and encourages and kisses the scraped knees and bruised feelings of the child. With that separation of roles, the job gets done. At least that is the old-fashioned model. Fortunately, for both the children and their fathers, this traditional model of the father as a "strong, silent type" is gradually losing ground. More young fathers are accepting their responsibility in the nurture of their children. More Dads are learning how to be motherly, and this is a positive development for the entire family. When a man learns that it is *not* unmanly to show affection, that he is *not* being soft or feminine when he expresses love in overt and emotional ways, both he and his children are the better for it.

Even when both parents are doing their share of the parenting, raising children can be a full-time job for two people. The division of roles between father and mother is, in that sense, a good thing. God designed the ideal human family to include two parents for a reason. There is great value in having both father and mother, each meeting a particular set of needs for the child. One supplies strength while the other gives comfort; one provides discipline while the other offers a softer kind of love—and then, from time to time, in healthy families, the parents' roles reverse somewhat.

But if effective parenting usually requires two earthly parents, it requires only one heavenly Parent. Our Creator combines the best characteristics of an earthly father and mother. He is both Mother and Father to us; He offers in one divine Parent all that two of us, working together, can give our natural children.

We are not accustomed to thinking of God as our heavenly Mother, but He in fact plays that role, too.

In several scriptural passages, God has referred to Himself in ways that suggest the maternal role more than the traditional paternal one. These are not common enough that we are likely to begin praying to "Our Mother, who art in heaven . . ."! But they do help us to see that God's parental attitude toward us includes the gentleness and the warmth which we often associate with motherhood. They emphasize the nurture of God, the softer and more accepting side of His feelings toward us.

Jesus Himself spoke of His motherly instincts toward us. In one moment of sorrow, as He wept for the people of Jerusalem and their spiritual blindness, He expressed not the outrage of an offended God, but the tender sadness of a mother unable to help a child she loves. "O Jerusalem, Jerusalem! . . ." He cried. "How often would I have gathered your children together as a hen gathers her brood under her wings, and you would not!" (Matt. 23:37, RSV).

Surely every Christian mother who has ever wept over a wayward child recognizes that emotion. Jesus is feeling the unique pain of a mother who aches to hold and protect her child. It is a familiar pain which only a mother—or a motherly God—can know.

The Old Testament contains other, happier expressions of the maternal side of our heavenly Parent. The psalmist David draws the word picture of God as a mother and himself as a contented baby in her arms: "Surely I have composed and quieted my soul; Like a weaned child rests against his mother" (Ps. 131:2, NAS).

In the opening verses of Isaiah, we see another

glimpse of God in a maternal role. "For the Lord hath spoken, I have nourished and brought up children . . ." (Isa. 1:2, KJV). It is also in Isaiah, near the end of the book, that we find what is perhaps the most engaging description we have of God as a Mother. God, speaking through the prophet, says to us: "And you shall be nursed, you shall be carried on the hip and fondled on the knees. As one whom his mother comforts, so I will comfort you . . ." (Isa. 66:12–13, NAS).

What a beautiful picture of God! We are the happy children of a Mother God who carries us, comforts us, fondles us on her knee. It is a far cry from the unfortunate vision of God as an angry and vindictive Enforcer which still persists in the minds of many.

God wants us to know that He is a Father who loves and cares and nurtures us—just like a Mother!

7

A Father Who
Chastens and Corrects

"My son, do not reject the discipline of
the Lord . . . For whom the Lord loves he reproves,
Even as a father, the son in whom he delights."
Proverbs 3:11–22, NAS

Discipline. There was a time, not so long ago,
when just the word made me want to run and hide.
As a member of a large family reared by old-
fashioned parents, I know about discipline.

My parents, heeding the biblical warning that
to spare the rod is to spoil the child, set out with
great determination to do neither. With twelve
children, administering even the most sorely needed
punishment required great diligence, several belts,
and a well-developed set of forearms. My parents
often assured me, as they set about their task, "This
hurts me worse than it hurts you." I never quite
believed it at the time.

My earliest memory of a full-scale, five-star
thrashing goes back to when I was in second grade.

FatherCare

My offense was misbehaving in church; my mistake was doing so in the presence, and within easy reach, of my father. During the morning worship service one Sunday, my older brother Phil pulled several pieces of candy from his pocket. I was sitting next to him, spotted the candy in his lap, and grabbed for it. He grabbed too. For a brief moment we engaged in a noisy tussle for the candy, forgetting that Dad was in the pew behind us. I was clearly the aggressor, and was making most of the noise. Dad stood up, leaned over the back of the pew, and yanked me bodily from my seat. He hoisted me over his shoulder, stepped from the pew, and marched grimly up the aisle, to the back of the church, and out the door.

He didn't say a word. I was stupid enough to fight over a piece of candy in the middle of a church service, but I wasn't too stupid to realize I was in big trouble. We lived two blocks from the church and did not own an automobile, so we walked, without breaking stride, out the church door, down the concrete steps, all the way home, and into the house without a single word being said.

Dad took me straight into the bedroom, bent me over the bed, took off his belt, and finally broke the silence. "You know what this is for, don't you, son?"

"Yessir," I said.

Whereupon he commenced. It was a memorable Sunday morning. That was only one in a long series of such occasions, in which both Dad and Mom took their turns at the job, and in which the work was done with switches or belts. The offenses ranged from simple misdemeanors to juvenile delinquency on a grand scale—the only thing all those childhood thrashings had in common is that I never got one I didn't richly deserve.

The word *discipline* evoked from me then, as from most people, memories of punishment—pain delivered for sins committed. But in the Bible the word usually bears a different connotation; it is typically more descriptive of the process of correcting, guiding, and teaching than of punishment. It is in this sense that God our Father is most often described as disciplining His children.

The two meanings are not entirely different, of course. There is in the punishment administered by most parents a large element of instruction. The good parent punishes to teach, to correct, to try to produce in the child a better behavior next time. Of all the times I was punished as a child, I do not recall an occasion in which the purpose was strictly punitive. The reference to the future was always there. The point was to improve future behavior, not just to punish past behavior.

No discussion of effective parenting can omit the subject of discipline. Good parenting always includes discipline. The growing child is by nature imperfect and undeveloped. The task of the parent is to guide that development, to point out to the child his errors, to reward his steps in the right direction, to teach him what is good. God, as a heavenly Parent, is obviously involved in such a disciplinary process with us. We, too, begin as children, with many lessons to learn. An accurate picture of God as Parent is complete when we see Him not only as providing for us and loving us, but disciplining us as we grow. That third part of the parental profile appears throughout the Bible.

"Thus you are to know in your heart," we read

in the Old Testament, "that the Lord your God was disciplining you just as a man disciplines his son" (Deut. 8:5, NAS). The same word picture occurs in the New Testament. In His message to members of the church at Laodicea, a "lukewarm" and wealthy church, God reminded them, "All those whom I love I correct and discipline" (Rev. 3:19, Phillips). In the epistle to the Hebrews is an explicit and detailed comparison of God's discipline with that of an earthly parent. Having described some of the difficulties which believers face, the author quotes Proverbs 3:11, then goes on to say:

"Bear what you have to bear as 'chastening'—as God's dealing with you as sons. No true son ever grows up uncorrected by his father. For if you had no experience of the correction which all sons have to bear you might well doubt the legitimacy of your sonship. After all, when we were children we had fathers who corrected us, and we respected them for it. Can we not much more readily submit to the discipline of the Father of men's souls, and learn how to live?

"For our fathers used to correct us according to their own ideas during the brief days of childhood. But God corrects us all our days for our own benefit, to teach us his holiness. Now obviously no 'chastening' seems pleasant at the time: it is in fact most unpleasant. Yet when it is all over we can see that it has quietly produced the fruit of real goodness in the characters of those who accepted it in the right spirit" (Heb. 12:7–11, Phillips).

The question of what God means by "chastening" those whom He loves has always been a perplexing one. Some people take the extreme view that the "chastening" of God is His punishment, that He sends tragedy into our lives to punish us for our sins, and hence to make us live more righteously. Even among presumably enlightened Christians, there is a temptation to think of the discipline of God in these punitive terms. An automobile strikes down a child, a heart attack comes suddenly and unexpectedly, a person suffers a tragic business reversal for no apparent reason—and the dark, lurking fear is that this is God's way of punishing us.

Such a view is logically inconsistent with what we know about God as a loving Father. Harold Kushner, in his recent book, *When Bad Things Happen To Good People*, addresses this misconception: "One of the ways in which people have tried to make sense of the world's suffering in every generation has been by assuming that we deserve what we get, that somehow our misfortunes come as punishment for our sins. . . . The idea that God gives people what they deserve, that our misdeeds cause our misfortune, is a neat and attractive solution to the problem of evil at several levels, but it has a number of serious limitations. It teaches people to blame themselves. It creates guilt even where there is no basis for guilt. It makes people hate God, even as it makes them hate themselves. And most disturbing of all, it does not even fit the facts."

The reference in Hebrews 12 to God's "chastening" His children does not seem to refer to discipline in a punitive sense at all, but to the process of instructing and guiding a small child. Not being a theologian, I have asked my former New-

Testament-Greek professor, Donald Bowdle of Lee
College, for a layman's explanation of the original
Greek word which is translated "chastening" in this
passage. The word used is *paideia* (transliterated),
and it is a form of the noun which means, literally,
"little child." The word refers to the type of
instructional discipline imposed on a child.
"Although the context may denote punishment,"
states Bowdle, "the words themselves have to do
with discipline in the sense of training and
instructing—the molding of character by reproof and
admonition."

We are all familiar with the kind of parental
discipline to which the author of the Hebrews
refers. This gentler type of correction is not so
dramatically remembered as those celebrated trips
to the woodshed, perhaps because it occurs so often.
A good parent corrects a child literally hundreds of
times; such correction is a part of the landscape of
the typical parent-child interaction. The parent must
play this role because a child learns by trial-and-
error. He has many things to learn, and he rarely
learns anything in one shot. The parent expects the
child to make mistakes; he expects to correct those
mistakes. And so with God.

Jesus engaged in this process with His
disciples. They repeatedly misunderstood what was
going on, and He patiently straightened them out.
Peter, one of Christ's favorites, was the worst of the
lot, and we see Jesus correcting Him probably more
often than any other disciple. Consider these
examples:

● Parents tried to bring their children to Jesus
to be blessed, and the disciples wouldn't let them

do so. Jesus corrected them: "Let the children come," He said.

● On the Sea of Galilee, when a storm blew up, the disciples panicked and accused Jesus of not caring about them. He patiently calmed the sea.

● When a crowd of five-thousand people were hungry and without food, the disciples could not understand what Jesus was doing about it. They recommended sending the entire mob away to scrounge for their own food. Jesus patiently explained to them.

● A Gentile woman from Syrophonecia came to Jesus asking for healing for her daughter. The disciples thought she was too loud, and wanted to throw her out. Jesus first corrected the disciples, then healed the woman's daughter.

● On the Mount of Transfiguration Peter, James, and John got so carried away with the glory of the moment that they wanted to build three monuments and stay forever. Jesus straightened them out, and even told them not even to talk about what had happened to anyone else.

● The disciples were "in school" right up until the very end of Christ's earthly ministry with them. At the Last Supper, they at first balked when He wanted to wash their feet. That night in the Garden of Gethsemane, supposedly helping Him keep vigil, they fell asleep. A few minutes later, when the soldiers came to arrest Jesus, Peter charged up to one of them and lopped his ear off; Jesus had to settle Peter down and put the man's ear back on his head. Then the disciples completed their fiasco by deserting Jesus, for fear of being arrested themselves. The disciples' behavior in that entire evening was a virtual comedy of errors, but Jesus never lost patience with them.

One could cite other stories in the Gospels of the disciples' constant need of correction and training, but the point is made. They had all the insight and spiritual depth of—well, of children! But apparently that is exactly what Jesus expected of them, and He responded with the patience and the gentle discipline of a kind father. These were the same men, of course, who would later prove themselves to be sturdy, mature leaders of the early church. They are the same men who showed such profound understanding of the mysteries of the kingdom, who wrote some of the epistles which became our Bible, who were the first martyrs of the faith. But that was later. First they had to begin just as you and I do, as children who need to be shown the way.

Henry Ward Beecher once said, "You cannot teach a child to take care of himself unless you will let him try to take care of himself. He will make mistakes. But out of these mistakes will come his wisdom."

God understands that for a child to learn to walk, he must fall a few times. A parent expects that and, when it happens, calmly picks up the child and sets him on his feet again, maybe with a quick kiss thrown in for good measure. Can't we expect our Father God to be as patient and gentle as He teaches us to walk the Christian walk? We need not fear that God expects us to do it perfectly the first time, that if we fall He will scathe us for our sins. His discipline is not that of the jailkeeper, or of the executioner. It is the discipline of the father.

8

God Chose a Family

"If God so loved us, we also ought
to love one another."
1 John 4:11, RSV

God lived on earth as a man.

That miracle of incarnation is a central fact of Christian theology. The mysterious fusion of God and man in Jesus Christ made all the later events of the crucifixion and resurrection meaningful.

"The Christian faith says [something] about the human predicament which no other religion comes within miles of saying," J. B. Phillips once wrote. "It is that God actually expressed himself in a man. Let us not smother this startling assertion by wrapping it up in a cosily familiar word like 'incarnation.' The truth is that God has been here on this planet, in person, and has assured us that all men and women are to be treated as his sons and daughters."

FatterCare

Mankind's redemption might conceivably have occurred in other ways, but God chose a method which involved a family. God, as Jesus Christ, took on the form not just of a human, but of a human *child.* He lived not just among men in a general sense, but specifically lived *in a family.* He knew the feelings of a child, the vulnerabilities of a child, the sense of smallness in a big, awesome world.

It would be wrong to suppose that God needs first-hand experience of a thing, in His earthly life as Christ, to understand it fully. As God, He can know all things without need of such specific experience. But it would also be wrong to dismiss as unimportant the specific, detailed arrangements by which God chose to accomplish man's redemption.

That God came as a little baby was not a random event. That He lived as a small child, that He experienced the nurture of a mother who was specifically picked for the role, that He had a father of emotional substance and integrity, in short, that He was a part of a *family*—none of that can be considered to be unimportant.

Theologians do not fully understand *why* God chose to live as a child, in a family, spending over half His earthly years in that role. I suspect there is a message there about the centrality of the family to the human existence which we have never fully comprehended. What we do understand is that God set up the human race into family units beginning with Adam and Eve. He Himself as Jesus became part of a family. He speaks of His interaction with us in terms of family relationships. The typology of the redemptive plan (being "born again") uses the concept of the parent-child experience as its figurative basis. The biblical explanation of God Himself as a Trinity involves the concept of Father and Son.

These are substantial indications that there is something about the family, and about the emotional and relational currents between parent and child, which is basic to the human experience on both a natural and spiritual level. And we can add to this evidence other hints which, though less weighty, fit the same pattern—for example, Christ's teaching His disciples to begin their prayers with "Our Father," or His statement in Matthew 19:14 about little children that "of such is the kingdom of heaven" (KJV).

An old Persian proverb says, "children are a bridge to heaven." Perhaps it is true. Perhaps in dealing with children, especially in relating as parents to them, we come closer to seeing clearly the ways of God with man than in any other of our natural relationships. Perhaps as parents we come as close to grasping the basic, primal urges of God toward us as the flesh will permit.

Chuck Colson, the White House attorney who found God in the aftermath of the Watergate scandal, describes in his book, *Born Again,* a telling incident that seems to suggest such a possibility. Colson relates an event in his life which occurred before he met God, at a time when he would have described himself as an atheist or agnostic, when he *thought* he did not believe even in the existence of God. He shares the story:

"I found myself remembering a curious shining moment seven years before. In the summer of 1966 I had bought a 14-foot sailboat for my two boys and hauled it to a friend's home on a lake in New Hampshire to teach them to sail. My son, then ten, was so excited over having his own boat that even though a gentle summer rain was falling the day of our arrival, he was determined to try it out.

"As the craft edged away from the dock, the only sound was the rippling of water under the hull and flapping of the sail when puffs of wind fell from it. I was in the stern watching the tiller, Chris in the center, dressed in an orange slicker, holding the sheet. As he realized that he was controlling the boat, the most marvelous look came over his cherubic face, the joy of new discovery in his eyes, the thrill of feeling the wind's power in his hands. I found myself in that one unforgettable moment quietly talking to God. I can even recall the precise words: 'Thank you, God, for giving me this son, for giving me this wonderful moment. Just looking into this boy's eyes fulfills my life. Whatever happens in the future, even if I die tomorrow, my life is complete and full. Thank you.'

"Afterwards, I had been startled when I realized that I had spoken to God, since my mind did not assent to His existence as a Person. It had been a spontaneous expression of gratitude that simply bypassed the mind and took for granted what reason had never shown me. More—it assumed that personal communication with this unproven God was possible. Why else would I have spoken unless deep down I felt that Someone, somewhere, was listening?"

Many of us have been nudged closer to God in moments spent with our children. It is as if the sensitivities between us and God and those between us and our children operate through similar channels, and the open flow of emotion and reflection in one channel stimulates the other. It is as if there occurs a kind of "sympathetic vibration"—that musical phenomenon in which the humming of one string in a musical instrument sets off a spontaneous vibration in another. There is a unique resonance in the affairs of parents and children that is similar in both the natural and the spiritual spheres.

It is little wonder, then, that the parent-child analogy is such a valuable way of thinking about God. It provides a structure within which God is more understandable, more approachable. It also suggests to us a way of relating to God which is emotionally satisfying as well as biblically sound. Referring to the parent-child metaphor helps us visualize God's qualities and reminds us of those characteristics of our own which should be cultivated.

The usefulness of this model goes beyond these obvious lessons, however, to illuminate other spiritual issues. We spoke earlier of the advantages of the parent-child analogy, citing its simplicity, its familiarity in virtually every culture, and its emotional richness. There is yet another attribute of this particular way of thinking about God: it can be used to shed light on a wide range of concerns in the kingdom. There seems to be an almost primal, basic quality about the interaction between parent and child which makes it applicable to a large variety of religious relationships. Let's take a look at three principles of the kingdom, all of which are better understood by application of the parent-child model.

FatherCare

Principle #1: Seeing ourselves as children in God's family encourages us to be more accepting of our spiritual siblings.

My daughters share a bathroom.

At twelve and thirteen years old, both have reached the age when the morning rituals of grooming and personal appearance are newly important. Each morning before they come down to breakfast, ready to board their school bus, the hair must be just right, the collars on the blouses turned up just so. Time spent before the bathroom mirror at that age is serious time—and for my daughters, it must be shared.

The sounds coming from that bathroom each morning are important signals of what kind of day it's going to be! The sounds are of two distinct varieties. As I pass my daughters' bathroom on some mornings, heading downstairs for my first cup of coffee, I hear the pleasant murmurs of two sisters in conversation, giggling over shared bits of silliness, whispering adolescent secrets back and forth—two sisters happily just being sisters as, side by side, they do whatever teenage girls do to get ready for school in the morning.

Those sounds are music to me. Hearing the spontaneous noise of two young girls sharing a bathroom holds more joy for me than the greatest symphony ever performed.

Unfortunately, there are those *other* days— mornings when the sounds from my daughters' bathroom give me no pleasure at all. On those days, the shared mirror and bathroom sink has somehow become a battleground. Who knows how the problems start? One girl wakes up grouchy, and the other soon becomes so. One is too slow, and the other too impatient. Maybe the shower runs out of hot water, or the curling iron is on the fritz, or someone wore someone else's sweater without asking—who knows? And does it matter?

On those mornings, on my way down to that first cup of coffee, I hear the noises of sisterly discord—the shouted accusations of this or that felony, the slamming of a bathroom cabinet door, even occasionally the sound of crying if matters have gotten truly out of hand. Nothing can ruin my morning as these sounds can. They discourage me. Just as the sounds of my daughters harmoniously passing the toothpaste have the power to warm and brighten my morning, so the sounds of their bickering over a hairbrush have the power to deflate even the most buoyant new day.

All parents can testify to the inordinate sensitivity we have toward fussing and fighting among our children. Whether it is the petty scrapes between two toddlers or the more serious conflicts between older teenagers, nothing is so sure to set our teeth on edge as strife and hard feelings between our children. I snap on the television in the morning and hear the news of bombings in Ireland, war in the Middle East, riots in Poland, and legislative infighting on Capitol Hill—but the total impact of all the accumulated strife around the world somehow doesn't affect me as much as that single fuss which I can hear going on in my daughters' bathroom!

It is this same parental sensitivity, of course, which causes us to take such great pleasure in our children's expressions of love for each other. Many times, when my children were roughhousing, playfully tussling with each other all over the floor or the furniture or the back seat of the car, I have allowed the fun to continue long past the point that it became too loud and too rambunctious, simply because I so enjoy seeing them enjoy each other. The responsible homeowner in me should stop the kids before they tear up the house, but sometimes the parent in me takes such great pleasure in seeing them play together that I am reluctant to call a halt.

I cherish those times when my child puts his arms around my neck to say, "I love you, Dad." But even more beautiful to me are the times when that child, spontaneously and naturally, offers to his sister or brother that same gesture of love. As a parent, is there any greater joy than to see two children whom you love deeply love each other?

I doubt it.

And so with God the Parent, whose household is a large and diverse one indeed. When we visualize the body of Christian believers as God's family, we can more clearly understand that the fragmentation and bitter competition within the church is a tragic and morally inexcusable condition. As a Father, God must necessarily be displeased by constant fighting within His household, and by the willingness of some of His children to exclude others from the family entirely.

I grew up in a church in which "Brother" and "Sister" were form of address used not just for clergymen, but for fellow members of the congregation as well. So common was this usage, and so exclusively were my childhood contacts limited to other church members, that until I

reached middle childhood I actually thought of
"Mr." and "Mrs." as rather foreign and exotic forms
of address. All the adults I knew were "Brother" or
"Sister" somebody.

When I became a teenager of the typically
rebellious sort, I grew rather contemptuous of the
"Brother Jones" routine, viewing it as an
embarrassing relic of my Pentecostal subculture. But
then, as I emerged from that stage of knee-jerk
rejection and moved into adulthood, I came to
understand the beauty of that small part of our
church's tradition. I can see now what symbolic
power that custom can have, and what a simple
spiritual truth it expresses. Calling one another
"Brother" and "Sister" is a small way for us to affirm
one another as fellow believers. It is a way of
reminding ourselves that, because we are all God's
little children, we are sister and brother to each
other.

We felt a strong sense of kinship in the church
of my youth. The people in that church did not call
one another "Brother" and "Sister" from habit
alone; they genuinely treated one another as
members of the family. There was a sturdy loyalty
within the church. We bought groceries from the
grocer with whom we worshiped—even if it meant
paying a bit more. We patronized the businesses
owned by our "brothers" and "sisters"—even if we
had to make a special effort to do so. We looked out
for our own. We were a family in that church, and
the glue that held us together was a strong feeling
that we were children of the same God. It was a
close, loving family of believers, and its influence on
me was enormous.

Unfortunately, there was another aspect of my

early church experience which was not so true to the biblical ideal. That local congregation richly nurtured me as a young boy, but it was part of a larger church denomination which held a narrow, severe definition of who was included in God's family. The church was so supportive to those of us *within* its family that we hardly cared that so many others were excluded—and on such trivial grounds. It is often the tendency of religious movements to become arbitrary and exclusive in their tests of fellowship. Country clubs or social fraternities may legitimately indulge in that sort of elitism, but those who claim to be the family of God must not!

My childhood church—which is still my church today—taught me many valuable lessons, but it did not give me an understanding of the breadth and scope of the family of God. As I grew older, I had to rethink the implications of what it means to have brothers and sisters in Christ, and to recognize my spiritual kinship with a far larger group of siblings than I ever knew existed. Many denominations and church bodies fail in similar fashion; it is more the rule than the exception. We practice various theologies of exclusion. Our evangelism sometimes is aimed at each other. We insist on emphasizing our many small differences more than our one, great, dominant similarity—that we are children of the same Father.

"By this shall all men know that ye are my disciples," Jesus tells us, "if ye have love one for another" (John 13:35, KJV).

Principle #2: Seeing ourselves as God's children helps us maintain a balanced attitude toward material prosperity and wealth.

There are few subjects in the church today which are more divisive than that of money. Viewpoints on materialism, honestly held by evangelical Christians, run the gamut. At one end of the continuum are those who believe it is wrong for Christians to accumulate middle-class comforts in a world where so many are hungry. At the other end of the spectrum are those who believe God wants everyone to be rich, and that material wealth is a *de facto* proof of divine favor. And of course there are dozens of more moderate views which lie somewhere between these two extremes.

The question seems not to be one of whether money is evil in itself; most of us will agree that money is merely a commodity and can be either good or evil, depending on its use. Nor is the question one of whether God desires for our necessary material needs to be met. Clearly He wants us to be well cared for, and He assures us He is concerned that our needs are provided. Neither is there disagreement over the means by which financial gain occurs; no one claims that the Lord approves of material gains which come from illicit enterprises of any sort.

The question is one of *how much is too much?* When should one suspect that, in the God-versus-Mammon struggle in his own life, Mammon may be gaining the upper hand?

Managing the stream of "goodies" which flow into a child's life is part of a parent's job. We like to see our children happy, but we understand that having every whim satisfied is not what produces happiness. The loudest and most animated conversations which ever occur in some households are discussions of such subjects as allowance, spending money, and whether Dad or Junior should pay for Junior's new pair of Levis. For a parent, the judgment calls can be difficult ones. We want our kids to have whatever they really need, but we don't want them to be spoiled little brats. One thing is sure: the good parent wants for his child whatever is best for him over the long haul—not necessarily what the child wants for himself right now. The parent knows that the way a child handles money and the values he learns from its use have far more importance than just the money itself.

Thinking about materialism in the context of the parent-child model helps keep the issue in a balanced perspective. First, it should help Christians avoid the neurotic fear of money as the Great Demon some feel it to be. *To propose that God disapproves of the accumulation of wealth for His children is simply to ignore a large body of scriptural evidence.* There is every reason to believe that God the Father applauds all those achievements of His children which are legitimately reached and which do not take the child away from fellowship with Him. Why should this be less true of achievement in financial areas than in academic, professional, athletic, or other pursuits?

God seems less concerned about the hazards of wealth than some of us are. He warns us of its limitations, but otherwise seems as willing for us to have large amounts of money as to have great talent, beauty, popularity, or professional skill. All these areas of human acquisition are limited; all are transitory; all are to be regarded as inferior to the truly spiritual qualities of the Christian life. Understanding that, we can pursue such goals with the confidence that God cheers us on, like a Little Leaguer's father with his son up to bat. God is not a jealous, insecure Neighbor who is threatened by our successes; He is a proud Father who takes pleasure in our achievement.

This parental attitude of God is as true towards financial success as towards other types of achievement. The Bible tells of wealthy men who found great favor with God—including David, Abraham, and Job. God specifically affirmed His approval of Job's massive—some might call it "excessive"—wealth by replacing it after Satan had stripped Job of it. The Bible speaks of God giving the ability to acquire wealth (Deut. 8:10), and in another place it offers a formula for material abundance (Prov. 3:9, 10). The apostle Paul, though himself not wealthy, says that one's bank account really is not what matters anyway: "I know what it is to be in need and what it is to have more than enough. I have learned this secret, so that . . . I am content, whether I am full or hungry, whether I have too much or too little. I have the strength to face all conditions by the power that Christ gives me" (Phil. 4:12–13, TEV).

Thinking of God as Parent suggests other implications of the materialism issue, however, beyond the basic truth that God can be pleased by

His children's financial success. Under what
conditions might natural parents *not* wish their
children to have more money or more of the things
money can buy?

Obviously, a parent would not want to give a
child money with which to finance an independence
for which the child was not prepared. Especially
during adolescence, when the disciplines and
constraints of the home are difficult to accept, it is
financial dependence on the parents which keeps
some kids from leaving prematurely. Would a loving
parent want his child to be able to financially afford
a course of action which would be damaging to his
overall development? Of course not.

Almost every adult male has at least one good
running-away-from-home story to tell, and mine is
pitifully brief and unexciting. I only tried it once, at
the age of eleven, and the excursion was so brief, so
halfhearted, that it hardly qualifies. I terminated my
escape plans so quickly that my parents didn't even
miss me. I was home before dark. As running-away-
from-home experiences go, mine was a total
bust, and I never even considered trying it again.
The truth is that as a child I was always broke,
totally dependent on my parents financially, and
leaving home was out of the question.

Being broke is not a noble reason for staying
home with Dad and Mom, but it's a common one
Dorothy Parker once quipped that "the best way to
keep children home is to make the home
atmosphere pleasant—and let the air out of the
tires!"

It is also possible, in a spiritual sense, for material

prosperity to create a climate in which individuals detach themselves from the care of their Father. In tougher times, leaning heavily on the Father's promises comes more easily, somehow. With "success" always comes an enlarged set of options. Money opens many doors, and some of them are the wrong doors, leading in directions God does not wish us to go. A loving God might well keep those doors closed if He knows we are not spiritually mature enough to handle the tough choices which material success brings.

Some children of God are bound to Him only by the urgency of life's pressures, by the sense that there are no options. In a foxhole, it is said, religion is about the best deal available. Prayer comes more easily then. The greater challenge to our genuineness as loyal sons and daughters comes when life is treating us well. "Better to turn to God," says the British writer Christopher Leach, "in times of intense vitality and sheer delight in the created world: to shout, rather than to plead." What God wants is for us to embrace Him at both ends of the fortune wheel, at the peaks and in the valleys, to have a constant love for Him as our Father whether we are broke or flush, beaten or on a winning streak.

The money—or fame or success or fortunes or love—should not be the thing; *He* should be the thing. Perhaps that is why Job is so highly praised in Scripture; his commitment to a loving sonship with God was there when he was rich, then when he was poor, then when he was rich—twice as rich, in fact—again. The money was not the big thing with Job; God was the big thing! And perhaps

knowing Job felt that way is what caused God to see
to it that, in the end, the money was there. Job
could handle it.

It seems apparent that not only would the
Father not want to be separated from His children
by their money; He also doesn't want money to
separate His children from each other.
    When I was five years old, the Sunday school I
attended had a contest. A five-dollar prize was to be
given to the youngest person who could recite the
Books of the Bible. Five dollars was big bucks in
those days, especially for a six-year-old. I had a
brother, Stephen, who was a year older than me,
and he set out to win the prize. He studied. He
memorized. He was drilled by Mom and Dad.
When the day of the contest came, Stephen was
ready. He could rip through the sixty-six books
without faltering, going from Genesis to Revelation
in one long machine-gun burst, stopping for breath
only twice—at Lamentations and Ephesians. He
could do it. And he was only six years old.
    The one obstacle in all this was me. I was five
years old, and the prize went not to the best or the
most deserving, but to the youngest. While Stephen
had been practicing, I had been listening. I could
hardly help it. We and two other brothers shared a
bedroom. The house had only one bathroom. The
whole family was crammed into that little house,
and we practically lived in each other's laps. When
Stephen memorized something, I *had* to memorize
it too. It was just there, in the air, to be acquired
through osmosis. So when time came for Stephen to
say the Books of the Bible in Sunday school that

morning, I waited for him to finish, then promptly stole his thunder *and* his five dollars by standing up after him and rattling off the chain of Bible names I had learned by hearing him practice. (I stopped for breath one extra time, at Malachi.)

I came home that day with more money than I had ever held in my hand at one time. This was 1951, when five dollars was five dollars. It seems cruel to describe a five-year-old child as "arrogant," but it is the only word that fits. Then Dad and Mom, in one of those parental edicts which leaves no room for disagreement, informed me that the five dollars would be divided equally between Stephen and me. Their reasoning was that we had both done the same work, achieved the same accomplishment, and thus deserved an equal reward. The $2.50 was still a lot of money to me, and I accepted their decree without tears, but it bothered me for years. Only when I became a father myself did I understand the parental instinct which produced that decision.

My folks understood the power that five-dollar-bill had to divide Steve and me. The posture of superiority which I was so inclined to assume that day would have persisted as long as the money lasted. The money would have been a potent symbol with the power to alienate. My parents did not begrudge me the five dollars, but they knew that the psychological dynamics which would have been set up between Steve and me by my having so much and his having none at all would have been destructive to our relationship. The inequity would have poisoned our interaction with each other and hence hurt both of us individually. We were two little boys, naturally competitive already, and we needed each other much more than either one of us needed five dollars.

Money has the power to divide, and God does not want it to divide His children. As we have discussed, it is not the money itself, but our attitude toward it, our use of it, which has such importance for our place in the family of God. For the believer who makes twenty thousand dollars a year to resent his Christian brother who makes two hundred thousand a year is obviously just as wrong as for the well-heeled to despise the poor. In either case, the fact that we are brothers and sisters is forgotten. The money becomes the issue. That is true materialism—a preoccupation with money to the neglect of the deeper and more important qualities. Materialism as a vice does not belong exclusively to the wealthy. It is just as big a problem with "have-nots" as with "haves."

God wants us to regard our kinship together in Him as the most important element of our interactions with one another. Whatever divides His children is, in that respect, a problem to be addressed, whether it is differences of race, nationality, politics, ecclesiastical label—or the size of our bank accounts.

Principle #3: God's parental style suggests that the church's first priority should be nurture.

The church has always had a challenge learning how to hate sin and love the sinner.

It is not an easy thing to manage. The church

must serve the function of both prophet and priest in the world; it must attack sin with prophetic zeal while befriending the sinner with priestly tenderness. The problem is one of where to place the emphasis. For the church, as for the believer, the problem is knowing where one crosses the line from tolerance and forgiveness into outright permissiveness. Or, from the other direction, where does a commitment to righteousness harden into an unloving legalism?

It is, of course, a question of balance, and referring to the parent-child model of God and man throws light on the issue.

A good starting place is a familiar parable in which Jesus placed God in the role of the Father and used a son to symbolize all of us:

"There was once a man who had two sons; and the younger said to his father, 'Father, give me my share of the property.' So he divided his estate between them. A few days later the younger son turned the whole of his share into cash and left home for a distant country, where he squandered it in reckless living. He had spent it all, when a severe famine fell upon that country and he began to feel the pinch. So he went and attached himself to one of the local landowners, who sent him on to his farm to mind the pigs. He would have been glad to fill his belly with the pods that the pigs were eating; and no one gave him anything.

"Then he came to his senses and said, 'How many of my father's paid servants have more food than they can eat, and here am I, starving to death! I will set off and go to my father, and say to him, "Father, I have sinned, against God and against you; I am no longer fit to be called your son; treat me as one of your paid servants.' " So he set out for his father's house.

"But while he was still a long way off his father saw him, and his heart went out to him. He ran to meet him, flung his arms around him, and kissed him. The son said, 'Father I have sinned, against God and against you; I am no longer fit to be called your son.' But the father said to his servants, 'Quick! fetch a robe, my best one, and put it on him; put a ring on his finger and shoes on his feet. Bring the fatted calf and kill it, and let us have a feast to celebrate the day. For this son of mine was dead and has come back to life; he was lost and is found.' And the festivities began" (Luke 15:11–32, NEB).

This parable gives us what is perhaps the best biblical illustration of how properly to balance forgiveness with a moral stand against sin. *In a proper balance, the tilt is emphatically on the side of forgiveness.* In this parable, greater value is placed on the human and personal needs of the individual sinner than on the maintenance of a public posture against any particular set of sins. In this moving story, God uses our own parental instincts to show us that human concerns dominate in such cases—that the abstractions of any ecclesiastical code are not as important as expressing love and acceptance to an individual who wants to come home to his Father.

We see several aspects of God's fatherliness in this story. First, we see the degree to which the father is emotionally vulnerable to the child. The child has the power to hurt his father, and in this case does so by rejecting him and by living a life contrary to his training. It is his love for the child that makes the father vulnerable. That is always the case with a parent's love: by loving the child, the parent places in the child's hand the power to hurt him. The greater the love, the greater the hurt. That is part of what being a good parent is all about.

I have a friend, Paul Duncan, who as dean of students at Lee College has the responsibility of campus discipline. He tells me that the toughest part of his job is informing parents that their children have seriously violated rules and are being expelled from school. These are usually Christian parents, good parents, who have sent their child off to a Christian college, only to learn that he or she is in trouble. There is no pain worse than that of a mother or father whose child, having been trusted and loved, disgraces himself. The parents are hurt—partially from their own sense of being betrayed, but mostly for the child they love.

The irony is that the parent hurts *because* he or she loves. An unconcerned parent feels no pain. By loving the child, the parent renders himself vulnerable to the potential hurt which the child by his behavior produces. That is the nature of parental love, and that is the nature of God's love for us. God is willing to hurt when we stray, if that is the price He must pay for loving us.

A second aspect of God's fatherliness seen in this story is that His is the kind of love which continues regardless of what we do. It is what psychologists call "noncontingent love"—that is, its presence does not depend on our loving in return, or behaving in a particular way, or anything else. It is just there. It is a part of God's parenthood. We are His children, so He loves us. Period. All the time the Prodigal Son was painting the town, all the time he was making a fool of himself in the big city, all the time he was wallowing in that pigpen, his father was loving him. Nothing he could do could stop his father's love. The father grieved. He stood by the road and hoped to see his son return, and he felt the pain that only a parent can feel. But he never gave up on loving his boy.

That is the message God wants us to get from this story: that His love is a constant, noncontingent, parental love.

To those churches or individuals which proudly erect elaborate hurdles over which people must leap to receive fellowship in God's family, the tale of the Prodigal Son is something of a rebuke. Some natural parents, in insisting that their children try to match their ideal model of the perfect child, communicate loudly and clearly to the child that he is not loved and accepted as he is, but must be virtually perfect in order to be valued. God the Parent does not do this. He gives His love to us *as we are*—then He points us toward what we can become. His love comes first, not later. It does not depend on our behavior, or even on our acceptance of the love itself.

If God is willing to love people as they are and to work on their problems as they go along, certainly the church should be no less accepting. We must not insist that such acceptance and discipline are mutually exclusive expressions of the church; both can and should exist. The question is rather one of priority: What shall the church say *first* to the individual? The model of parental love shows us that *first* comes the nurture then comes the training.

There is in developmental psychology a way of looking at parental styles called the "Schaeffer circumplex model," which suggests that the two major dimensions of parenting are Nurturance and Control. Nurturance includes all the parental expressions of care, love, acceptance, and positive attention. Control includes the setting of limits, establishment of rules, and general exercise of parental authority. The various combinations of high and low levels of Nurturance and Control have been studied to determine how they contribute to (or detract from) the development of healthy personality in children.

The major principle which runs throughout the various Schaeffer findings is simply this: that the parent can impose a high level of Control *if* he also provides high levels of Nurturance. Lots of love plus lots of discipline is a good combination, it seems. The negative side effects of too much authority occur only when that authority is not accompanied by an equivalently high level of Nurturance.

That insight into natural parenting has obvious implications for the church. If the standards of biblical holiness are to be taken seriously by a church, they must be taught in an atmosphere of loving, accepting spiritual nurture. When a church is accepting of an individual only to the extent that he or she meets their standards of behavior, that church misses the whole point of God's fatherliness, of his unrelenting, noncontingent love.

9

When I Grow Up . . .

"We are no longer to be children . . . we are
to grow up in all aspects into Him."
Ephesians 4:14–15, NAS

The most profound truths are rarely one-sided.
The greatest principles of life, like double-edged
razor blades, usually cut in two directions. Truth
often comes packaged as paradox.

An attempt to explain Christian discipleship by
use of any single analogy must keep that point in
mind.

The analogy of the disciple as a child of a
heavenly Parent, rich as it may be, is incomplete if
not extended to include an emphasis on the
characteristics of Christian maturity. The child does,
after all, eventually grow into an adult, and as he
does, he changes. Behavior once accepted as
appropriate is no longer tolerated. The normal
characteristics of a healthy child change, or we

begin to feel that something is badly wrong. What we call "cute" in the six-year-old is irritating in the ten-year-old, and in the sixteen-year-old is cause to call in the psychiatrists.

The apostle Paul uses this very fact to make a point in one of his letters: "When I was a child, my speech, feelings, and thinking were all those of a child; now that I am a man, I have no more use for childish ways" (1 Cor. 13:11, TEV).

Growing up is such an obvious and natural result of childhood that most children can hardly wait to get there. They seem determined to escape childhood as soon as possible, and the closer they get to adulthood, the faster they want to move. Their eagerness to be "adult" is so apparent that we parents sometimes use it to prod our children into better behavior. "Why don't you act your age?" we ask in exasperation when they behave badly. "When will you *ever* grow up?" "You're being *so* immature!"

Sound familiar? Those expressions thrown at a child are the most lethal arrows in the adult's quiver because they hit such a sensitive target; they cut sharply because of the constant desire of children to be a bit more grown-up than they actually are at any given time. That desire is natural because the process of moving toward adulthood is natural. It is an inexorable, compelling part of childhood.

Being like a child is necessary for living in God's kingdom, but there are also some very *un*childlike qualities toward which Scripture points us. "Be a child," God tells us. "But grow up!" the Bible adds. The emphasis in this book has been on the scriptural reminders to be childlike, but one of the attributes of childhood itself is the push toward maturity, and that emphasis is in the Bible too.

The apostle Peter called on the believers to whom he ministered to "grow in the grace and knowledge of our Lord and Savior Jesus Christ" (2 Pet. 3:18, NAS). His words make it clear that he had in mind, as he wrote, exactly the analogy which we are using now. "Like newborn babes," he urged them, "long for the pure milk of the word, that by it you may grow" (1 Pet. 2:2, NAS).

When the apostle Paul wrote to the Christians in Corinth, he used the same word picture to speak to them of their own development: "And I, brethren, could not speak to you as to spiritual men, but . . . as to babes in Christ' I gave you milk to drink, not solid food; for you were not yet able to receive it" (1 Cor. 3:1–2, NAS).

In another place, Paul challenged the members of the church at Ephesus to move past spiritual childhood. It is interesting that this great Christian, in making the challenge, included himself. "We are no longer to be children," he said, "tossed here and there by waves, and carried about by every wind of doctrine, by the trickery of men, by craftiness in deceitful scheming; but . . . we are to *grow up* in all aspects into Him. . . ." (Eph. 4:14–15, NAS, emphasis mine).

A central feature of childhood is that it is a time of constant growth. Maturity is progressive development in a positive direction. It is more than merely adding years to one's age; one can become older without necessarily becoming more mature.

To the child of God, maturity means growing in the direction of God Himself, becoming more like the perfection which only God achieves, but toward which we are told to reach. *To be like Jesus* is the goal of the maturing believer.

Being like God occurs as a result of two different processes: the "genetic" kinship which occurs at the new birth, and the modeling which continues, consciously and unconsciously, after one's birth into God's family. In the natural sense, we see the same two processes at work, and together they can produce children who are very much like their parents. Genetically, children bear certain similarities to their parents by virtue of being their offspring. These qualities we inherit; they pass to us automatically. The child need not do anything at all to have the same color of skin, hair and eyes as his parent. The same is true of size, bone structure, and even facial appearance. When we are born, we are already "like" our parents to a certain extent, not as a result of anything we do, but simply because of whose child we are.

In the experience of the new birth, similarly, we automatically assume certain properties of God and become "like Jesus" by virtue of God's redemptive work. In a manner analogous to that of genetic transfer, we assume a kinship to God which cannot be gained by any amount of deliberate effort to copy or imitate God.

Much of the similarity between parents and their children, however, do not result from automatically inborn qualities, but develop gradually over the years, as the child spends time with that parent, exposes himself to the parent's influence, and absorbs the parent's style and personality. Most of the similarity between parents and child, by far, is due to this process. If you walk like your father walks, it may have to do in small part to the structure of your hip and pelvic bones, but it is much more likely to be a result of having watched him walk during all the early years when you were taking your own first steps. Talking like your mother talks is more likely a result of being around her than of having a similar vocal apparatus.

Becoming like God is likewise more a result of imitation and modeling than it is of the new birth alone. All new Christians have that initial likeness to Him which He imparts. Whether one goes on from there to become more mature, to be more like Jesus, is up to the individual Christian, and that is why we see such wide variation among believers on the maturity dimension.

Psychologists distinguish between conscious, deliberate copying of another person's behavior, (which they call "imitation"), and the process of unconsciously taking on the qualities of another person, (which is called "modeling"). Both processes operate between parent and child to make the child similar to his parents.

The Bible suggests that both imitation and modeling are also important in our spiritual lives. "As children copy their fathers you, as God's children, are to copy him," says the apostle Paul in Ephesians 5:1 (Phillips). Jesus, speaking of His relationship with God the Father, once told His disciples: "I assure you that the Son can do nothing of his own accord, but what he sees the Father doing. What the Son does is always modeled on what the Father does" (John 5:19, Phillips).

Specific imitation of the behavior of Christ is

exactly what is proposed in the book, *In His Steps,*
the Charles Sheldon novel which has been a major
influence in the Christian community for almost a
hundred years. This approach can provide a basis for
daily decision making, using the historical example
of Jesus as the model, as suggested by 1 Peter 2:21:
"Christ . . . suffered for you, leaving you an
example, that you should follow in his steps" (RSV).
Imitation, however, though a worthy principle, is
difficult to utilize as a practical matter because of
the sheer time and distance which separate us from
the historical Jesus. Imitating Him requires us to
make inferences as to "what would Jesus do in this
situation." And, because we were not actually
present when Jesus walked the earth, such
inferences are necessarily speculative.

The process of modeling, in contrast to
imitation, occurs without the child's conscious effort.
He does not try to be like the parent; rather, his
behavior and personality are subtly shaped to
resemble the model. The child usually is not even
aware the process is taking place. Developmental
psychologists have specified several conditions which
make modeling more likely to occur, and make it
more powerful and permanent in the experience of
the child. These conditions include: (1) the degree
of similarity which the child perceives as existing
between him and the model, (2) the overall level of
competence and skill which the model demonstrates
to the child, and (3) the amount of time spent in the
presence of the model.

If indeed these conditions are perfect for
modeling, the stage is set for a child of God to

become more and more like the Father through a rich, constant modeling experience.

The first of these conditions is beautifully met by the incarnation. By becoming a flesh-and-blood human person, God removed Himself from the realm of abstraction and became a personal "model-able" God. He made it possible for us to become more like Him by identifying with Him. We *can* perceive the similarity between ourselves and the Jesus Christ we read about in the Gospels. We see Him as being like us to the extent that modeling His behavior is a coherent idea to us. The Bible encourages that perception; speaking of Christ, the Scripture tells us that "he also came a human being. . . . It is plain that for this purpose he did not become an angel; he became a *man*, in actual fact a descendent of Abraham. It was imperative that he should be made like his brothers in every respect . . ." (Heb. 2:14, 16–17, Phillips).

The second condition for good modeling—the competence of the model—is also met when the incarnate Christ is our model. No fact of biblical history is better documented than the total mastery which Jesus exercized while on earth. He dominated every situation He was in, whether by miracles or by the quiet power of His presence. He was always in total control—of Himself, of those around Him, even of the forces of nature itself. In Christ we have a model who is both like us and vastly superior to us. That is a virtual recipe for optimal modeling.

The final element—time spent in the presence of the model—is entirely up to the child of God. The Father is always there; it is *we* who must make

time for *Him.* In growing toward Christian maturity,
there is no substitute for time spent with the
Father. Without it, growth in the right direction is
impossible. Time spent with God may take the form
of prayer, Bible reading, worship, private reflection,
or even a long walk in the woods or a long evening
in front of the fireplace with Him. All the miracles
of the incarnation and all the demonstrations of
Christ's mastery will not result in one iota of
Christlikeness in us if we do not ourselves take time
with the Father.

Have you ever noticed how little children want
to "connect" with their parents the very first thing
every morning, as soon as they wake up. When my
children were small (and even now on an occasional
lazy Saturday morning), my wife and I were
accustomed to having "visitors" in bed with us early
every day. The kids enjoyed starting the day by
piling into bed with us and snuggling down for a few
minutes. We had a crowded bed lots of mornings,
with two sleepy adults and three giggly little
children. The first thing they wanted to do every
day, it seemed, was to make contact with their
father and mother.

I believe our Father God would be pleased by
such an attitude from us. He would like us to
awaken every day eager to connect with Him and
start the day by talking with Him. There are hints
in Scripture that Jesus did just that—as well as
David in Old Testament times.

Early or late, the point is to spend enough time
in the presence of the Father that the modeling
effect takes place, naturally, and we gradually come
to be more and more like Him. Spiritual maturity

will occur only in that fashion. The maturing process cannot be forced; it will not happen overnight. It will not occur automatically, by the sheer passage of time. We must create the conditions for growth, then trust that the growth is proceeding within us as we talk with God, read His Word, and seek to do His will.

5/14

80√